CANTERBURY LETTERS TO THE FUTURE

THE MOST REVD AND RT HON GEORGE LEONARD CAREY, 103rd Archbishop of Canterbury, was born in 1935. He worked in an office and did his National Service in the RAF before his innate delight in reading and serious study led him naturally to an academic career; and his strong sense of vocation to the priesthood.

He studied for his BD at London University, and then for his MTh while serving his curacy at St Mary's, Islington. He was awarded his PhD during his first two academic posts at Oak Hill Theological College and St John's, Nottingham. He has written ten books on aspects of theology ranging from the popular to serious work on Christian apologetics, and including major studies of the Atonement, Christology and the doctrine of the Church. His well-known account of the transformation of a city-centre church, *The Church in the Market Place*, grew out of his time as Vicar of St Nicholas', Durham. From here he moved to become Principal of Trinity College in Bristol, becoming an Hon Canon in 1984. During this period he served on General Synod and some of its major committees, work which continued when he became Bishop of Bath and Wells in 1987. He is a Fellow of King's College, London.

George was a keen sportsman in his youth, but is now more of an armchair supporter, particularly of Arsenal FC. He met his wife, Eileen, when they were both worshippers at Dagenham Parish Church in 1960 and she has fully shared in his ministry. They have four children and delight in their seven grandchildren, to whom this book is dedicated.

DEDICATED TO MY GRANDCHILDREN

Simon, David, Oliver, Jonathan, Edward, Joseph and Emily

'Trust in the Lord with all your heart
and lean not on your own understanding;
in all your ways acknowledge him,
and he will make your paths straight'
Proverbs 3:5–6

Canterbury Letters to the Future

GEORGE CAREY

KINGSWAY PUBLICATIONS
EASTBOURNE

ISBN 0 85476 773 8

Designed and produced by Bookprint Creative Services
P.O. Box 827, BN21 3YJ, England for
KINGSWAY PUBLICATIONS
Lottbridge Drove, Eastbourne, E Sussex BN23 6NT.
Printed in Great Britain.

Contents

Preface

This book began with the best of intentions some ten years ago, shortly before I became Bishop of Bath and Wells. It was then that I decided to write a book on Christian doctrine for lay people. Arising from my experience as a parish minister, and later as Principal of Trinity Theological College, I concluded that there was need for a serious book outlining the substance of Christian theology that did not underestimate their intelligence nor overestimate their knowledge of technical theology.

Inevitably the unexpected invitation to become an English diocesan bishop was enough to put the project on the back burner, although I made valiant efforts, whenever spare time appeared, to keep faith with my commitment. Then, in 1990, my appointment as Archbishop of Canterbury seemed at the time to represent the final *coup de grâce* to my good intentions. But even then something within me refused to give up. In spite of the demanding responsibilities as Archbishop of Canterbury I was reluctant to throw up my hands in despair, because this book was consonant with all I stood for as a leader within God's Church to 'feed the flock of Christ'. I had entered into a promise with my publishers and promises should always be kept.

By 1995 I had written sixteen rough chapters, but time to refine them into a state that would satisfy me and the general public still seemed as elusive as ever. As the demands of my office grew greater, so spare time seemed to diminish. That the job is complete I owe to two special women whose contributions to this book are immense. First, I gladly cite Eileen, dearest friend and devoted wife. She encouraged me when my resolve weakened and reminded me constantly that 'once I had put my shoulder to the plough . . .'. It was Eileen who first put into my head the idea to write a book for my grandchildren. Words cannot adequately express what I owe to her and her love over the years.

Then in 1995 another remarkable woman came to my rescue, Dr Ruth Etchells. My friendship with this remarkable scholar and theologian goes back to the early 70s when we first met in Durham. Her own rich writings, inspired by English literature, nourished by faithful attention to Christian theology and quickened by a sharp attentive intelligence, have always appealed to me. Indeed, at my request she wrote one of the best Archbishop of Canterbury's Lent Books *Set My People Free* (1996) which challenged the Church to re-evaluate its attitude to the role of lay people. Ruth, recently retired, was more than willing to take my sixteen chapters and to work with me in preparing them for publication. And this she has done with enormous skill, patience and dedication. Both of us have had to find extra time in busy diaries to meet often, and both of us have found it an exciting time to share ideas about the faith that still yields so many wonderful discoveries. Thank you, Ruth, for the immense gift of yourself. Nevertheless, the book is mine and I gladly take responsibility for any faults that remain.

One of the challenges in writing a book like this is knowing what to leave out. Readers will quickly note that some very important doctrines are missing, namely those concerned with the Church – its nature, its sacraments, ministry and mission. These are all outworkings of God's dealings with us and our corporate response to him. While in my original sixteen chapters I had considered the life and ministry of the Church, as Ruth and I revised the work, it became clear that this material effectively constituted a second volume. There were so many things to be said first, about God and the world! So, though with regret, the detailed study of these further doctrines I have left for a future day, when I am able to look back on all I have learned, from my particular vantage point, of the inner meaning and theological richness of the Church and her life.

There are others I must thank. My grateful thanks to Richard Herkes of Kingsway Publications for his friendship and forbearance. He too never gave up waiting and hoping. Appreciation is due also to Canon Colin Fletcher, friend and Chaplain, who has been of enormous help and encouragement, as have been other members of my loyal team at Lambeth and Canterbury. Finally, many references will be found in this book to the Anglican Communion to which I belong. I am proud to be part of this suffering, fallible, struggling and glorious body. It tells me that wherever suffering faith and loyal commitment meet with the grace and power of God, from that alchemy surprising things emerge which under God will prove a dynamic 'Faith for the Future'.

George Carey
Canterbury
September 1997

INTRODUCTION

To the Future

It all began with children. I remember it well: 29th December, St Thomas's Day. The day in the Church's calendar when we remember one of the most famous of archbishops, Thomas Becket, struck down by four knights in his own cathedral on 29th December 1170. A day, inevitably, when any current archbishop is drawn to reflect on the past he has inherited, in both its tragedy and its greatness.

The first commemorative service was over, and now it was early afternoon. Our family lunch in the Old Palace at Canterbury had just finished. I was sitting in the window of the lounge looking onto the glorious West Front of the Cathedral. The day was bright and there were some local children playing in front of the great door of the magnificent building. Behind me my own grandchildren, Simon, David and Oliver, were also playing merrily, while the two youngest members of the family, Jonathan and Edward, were being fed by their young mothers, my daughters. At that moment the world belonged to the children . . .

And the powerful contrast struck me, between the scene I was at that moment watching, and the events of 1170, to say nothing of the unbroken line of Archbishops of Canterbury that goes back fourteen hundred years to the coming of Augustine in AD 597. Suddenly I was aware in a fresh way, palpably aware, of the line of 102 predecessors whose mantle had now fallen on me. While, in these children, the future was already being written.

No Archbishop of Canterbury can escape the responsibility of the history he has inherited. But neither can he – should he – be so aware of and answering to the past that his mind is looking backward more than forward. 'Is it not,' I mused, 'something of a temptation to be reflecting too much on the past?' In the Church we so often seem to be looking back to (supposed) 'golden ages' when faith was bright, even if life was not always secure. But was it ever really so simple? Each period of our Church's history speaks of tragedy and triumph mixed, of cowardice and courage, fear and faith. Who could consider the faith of the same Augustine, first Archbishop of Canterbury, without reflecting also on his considerable fear and uncertainty – enough almost to turn him back – on his way to Britain?

It was then I decided that I wanted, as the current archbishop, to address the future represented by those children I was watching that bright December afternoon. I wanted to write some 'Letters to the Future', to the *adult* Simon and David and their contemporaries now playing so happily in these precincts. To Oliver, now three years old, who will be a mature fifty-five in the year AD 2050, and to his generation. To write to them from *my* generation of the 'things we have most surely believed', the Christian faith which, inherited from the past, we have made our own. For, testing it in the fires of this century, we have discovered for ourselves its marvellous power.

But let me position myself in this story and why I am approaching this book in this way. I write as a successor of the fearful, faithful Augustine, from my own time, from the dying years of a century which began in such ambition and hope, which has achieved such astonishing developments, and which yet has to confess suffering and cruelty on a global scale. During it we have swung between the achieving of extraordinary feats, the exhibiting of most noble capacities of the human spirit and the sounding of appalling depths of evil. H. D. Carberry wrote halfway through this century:

> I think they will remember this as the age of lamentations
> the age of broken minds and broken souls . . .
> The age of failure of splendid things.
>
> And yet, deep down, an age unsatisfied by dirt and guns.
> An age which though choked by the selfishness of the few
> who owned their bodies and their souls,
> still struggled to the end,
> And in their time reached out magnificently
> Even for the very stars themselves.

The Church too has itself experienced failure as well as achievement during this century, and has much to grieve about. There has been shame as well as glory in the Church's calling to stand alongside men and women, with joy in their achievements, with suffering in their grief, with challenge in times of corruption. In my travels across the world, visiting the family of the Anglican Communion, I have seen the tension of achievement and horror with my own eyes. I cannot forget driving through Bombay, seeing new buildings rising on all sides and the

roads crowded with new BMWs, yet there on the pave-
ments naked children begging from passing strangers.
Nor can I escape from the haunting look in the face of the
young Sudanese woman in that refugee camp outside
Khartoum begging me, yes, pleading with me for help to
return to her home. As a representative of Christ's Church
I stood there alongside her in her desperation. And I
shared some of it, for I could not offer her what she longed
for. No words are adequate for my own sense of helplessness at her plight, and my anger at evil systems which
condemn young people to futile existences in desert
camps.

Helplessness and anger; two responses widely experienced by those who work for the betterment of things.
And this has been true not only in the more dramatic
crises of the two-thirds world but in the affluent West. For
we have been conscious of many things deeply wrong in
our corporate lives, and felt helpless and frustrated when
trying to amend them. Behind that lies a sense of the loos-
ening of those values in our own Western society which
over the centuries have bonded us together. We are less
certain of what 'betterment' is, even of what 'right' and
'wrong' actually mean. For if our nation has to some
extent left behind – or at least called into question – the
Biblical Ten Commandments (up to thirty years ago read
every Sunday in all Anglican churches) we are by no
means sure what should take their place, and our media
are constantly prompting debate on the subject.

But that, in fact, takes us to the real issue. The sharpest
difference between any 'commandments' proposed for
today in response to this debate, and the original ones, is
not so much in their content – what they say – as in their
origin – who originates and authorises them. For contemporary 'commandments' are seen as 'commanded' only

by the consensus of society; whereas the Biblical Ten Commandments were understood as the expression of a relationship between a people and the Lord God, and therefore underwritten by divine revelation and sanction. And for Christians this understanding has not changed; but it has developed. For Christians believe that the sense of living in relationship with God, expressed so vividly in the Old Testament and encapsulated in the Ten Commandments, was definitively re-expressed for humanity in the unique life of Jesus Christ – in his teaching, in his death and resurrection. And more than merely 're-expressed', that relationship with God moved on, developed into something continuous with the past but infinitely richer. The encounter of humanity with God through Jesus Christ shaped a wholly new understanding of who God is and what he desires for us and effects for us. So what was handed on by those first followers of Jesus, who in turn shared their beliefs and experiences with those who succeeded them, was not discontinuous with the Ten Commandments and the relationship with God that lay behind them, but was a new and deeper relationship with God which challenged people to a different order of living.

'Handed on' I said. Yes; right to our own time; and so into yours, by people like me. In spite of the twists and turns of history and cultural expression which have necessarily been a feature of the way the Church has interpreted it, at its core that faith remains the same: the faith concerning how God 'is' in relation to us and to the world; and how we 'are' in relation to him. That is the faith we have received from those who have gone before us and which we Christians of the late twentieth century have lived by; that faith which we now hand on to you who are to come; to you, our fellow Christians of the future, and, our dear brothers and sisters, in a common obedience to Jesus Christ.

So these Letters written from the chair of St Augustine and also from the humble life experience of your fellow Christian George, with all the blemishes of ordinary fallibility and struggle, are an attempt to share with you of the future the essentials of our faith; they offer you the certainties of the God of whom our faith speaks even in the midst of all the uncertainties with which the nature of our times and their philosophies inevitably challenge us. We Christians of this time and space have found that faith is shaped in four ways: it is anchored in the Bible; taught by the Church; probing of every human culture; and always relevant to the way we should live. In order to help you stand the testing of your own times, I want to set out the great things of our faith in their coherent pattern as it is revealed by that fourfold shaping; a pattern which has to be articulated and owned by each generation. Every part of that pattern is vital to the strength and power of that faith.

So, in my first Letter we shall begin to look at what these fundamentals are and how we should approach them; and how they may thrillingly empower the life of the Church and of its individual members. Indeed, how they have done so through the centuries, and will, I am wholly certain, do so in your own lives.

As my story unfolds you may well be surprised by the things that have concerned us and the storms that have sometimes blown us off course. I fear they may even seem trivial in comparison to the problems and issues that you may have to address. Nevertheless, for your time as for mine, the same struggle to articulate the faith of Jesus Christ will be paramount. And in order that what follows may stand the testing of your own times, we need to set out the great things of our faith in their coherent pattern; a pattern which has to be articulated and owned. It is called Christian theology. How vital that is to the strength of our faith, and what are its fundamentals, must be the content of my first Letter.

LETTER 1

Ways of Thinking About God

Dear Friends of the Future,

What are you of the future being invited to read, I wonder? My generation has well and truly embarked upon the electronic revolution. I would love to know what advances in learning you are enjoying. Whatever the methods, for Christians of all ages the task remains the same – to learn about the faith and to make its riches one's own.

When I was a young enquirer myself, already committed to Jesus Christ but greenly ignorant about the faith, I was plied with book after book on Christian things. They fell into two groups: the first retold me a simple faith which undoubtedly nourished me to begin with, like a baby on bland premixed food, but they seemed to ignore or deny that there were any questions which should be asked, or problems to be faced, for believing Christians. So in the end they could not satisfy. I felt like those early Christians in Corinth whom Paul challenged as being merely 'milk-fed' because they were not ready for solid food (1 Corinthians 3:2). I had to make the same transition, as every thoughtful and maturing Christian must, that Peter made at Caesarea Philippi, from simple belief to a profounder doctrinal understanding; from simply 'following', to being able to discern, at increasing depth, theological truth: 'You are the Christ, the Son of the living God' (Matthew 16:16).

The second group of books I was offered helped me in that direction, challenging me to think as carefully and rigorously as I could about this faith I had made my own, by identifying questions and recognising not only the inevitable uncertainties, but the competing claims of other faith systems and ideologies, and exploring in what way the Christian faith addressed them. However, I found the problem often with this group of books was their failure to come with the same sense of excitement and commitment to faith that the first group of books undoubtedly did. I have remained profoundly convinced ever since that any book which aims to give a convincing answer for the hope that is within us, must be true to the four fundamental elements of Christian theology. I touched upon this fourfold structure at the end of my Introduction. For Christian theology is *that discipline which seeks to give a coherent statement of the Christian faith which is anchored in the Bible, taught by the Christian Church, related to our culture and relevant to the way we live.*

The faith I want to hand on to you as tested in the struggles we have experienced in the twentieth century had to be grounded and explored in those fundamental ways. Let me expand a bit on why they are each important.

The need to be Biblical

True Christian theology will always be anchored in the

teaching of Scripture, and will not depart from it. It should be possible of any doctrine to see its Biblical basis even where Christians may disagree concerning the importance or even the value of the teaching in question. Valid Christian doctrine is never the result of intellectual speculation divorced from the Biblical roots of our faith.

But, in insisting on this, we are aware of a number of dangers. There is, for instance, the danger of merely paying lip-service to it. It is dangerously possible to treat the Bible as a kind of wax nose which we push into position to suit the shape of our argument. So we must constantly test the honesty of our engagement with Scripture, asking of any Biblical material we are deploying to support our views: 'Does it really say that or mean that?' The use of the cultural context is critical here. In our times we have been much engaged in discerning what Biblical statements might mean in the context of their own culture on the one hand, and, on the other, how they speak to our own present culture. We are conscious, you see, that we inevitably filter our understanding through minds that are shaped by the culture we live in.

So it is vital that we bring both knowledge and imagination to bear in understanding and acknowledging what was being said at the time it was said, rather than inadvertently reading our own culture back into it; or worse, regarding our own times as superior to those in which the material was written, and so letting them control and limit our understanding.

The two words which have been a key for us to getting all this rightly balanced are, first, 'interpretation' – that is, the process by which our hearts, minds and wills decide what this passage means and what it reveals about Christian truth. And, second, 'hermeneutics', a more technical word which, though it comes from a root meaning 'to interpret', describes a rather different operation. Hermeneutics goes to the very heart of the difference between Biblical times and ours, asking, 'When we read so-and-so, does it mean what our use of those words would mean today?' For instance, when we ponder the Bible's teaching about eschatology, that doctrine of the Last Things which speaks of heaven, hell and judgement, it is clear that incorporated within that teaching are first-century views concerning cosmology. Such a 'three-decker' universe of hell below, present existence on earth, and heaven above obviously does not belong to the conceptual framework of our lives in the twentieth century. And who knows what cosmology will be yours in the twenty-first? Certainly something far more sophisticated than ours, if developments in both knowledge and theory, happening even now as I write, reshape and expand your thinking as ours has had to be. So, how does one interpret the truth of eschatology when its physical details must be largely discarded? Our study of hermeneutics has helped us to deal with the meaning of doctrine when the framework in which a Biblical truth has come to us is culturally shaped.

And then again, not only can Scripture be minimised or misappropriated culturally, it can also be misused by failure to understand the complexity of its form. The Bible is a complex collection of documents, hymns, stories, prayers and discourses which came together over a period of more than a thousand years from, say, 900 BC to AD 100. For the last two hundred years or so of modern times, it has been subjected to the most rigorous and detailed analysis, and the fruits of this research must profoundly affect our understanding of what the Bible says. It is not possible for a serious Biblical student to ignore this scholarship, and indeed it would be a sad deprivation for such a student to try to do so. Unfortunately, as we conclude this century in which such great steps have been taken in Biblical scholarship, we still have some preachers and Christian leaders among us who appear to ignore the rich scholarship and learning built up over this period of time, and who therefore do not take into consideration as they prepare to proclaim the Biblical faith, the culture or the background or the particular situation which gave birth to the passage of Scripture they are expounding.

And, I regret to say, far from honouring Scripture this does it a grave disservice. I have myself been moved, through experience and grace, to a high doctrine of the Bible. I believe it is God's Word, and so declare it to you. I want you to know that. When we study it and listen to what it has to say, God himself speaks through it to challenge, feed and encourage us. But it is also a book which has come through ordinary men and women inspired by the Spirit of God. There are human aspects of divine writing, and by comparing scripture with scripture, and listening to theologians of the past as well as the present, we can distinguish those sections of the Bible which have fulfilled their day from those which address our day with immediacy. For example, unlike strict Jews, Christians do not feel it necessary to keep the food laws of the Old Testament, because Christ has fulfilled the Law of Moses. Furthermore, we also do not feel – even in our own violent twentieth-century culture – that it would be right for us to massacre the occasional Amalekite, because we have recognised, as you in your times will recognise, that the New Covenant through Jesus Christ requires us to walk in love and peace with all people. This weighing up of the eternal truth with which the Bible addresses us, recognising in it those things immediate to our faith and

those things which have been part of its temporal history,
is an essential part of thinking about our faith theologically. For taking into account all the complexities I have
touched on here, we have still found the Bible to remain
the ultimate yardstick of theology, the measure against
which we assess the truth or error of doctrine.

Taught by the Church

In my century it was Cardinal Suenens who said so splen-
didly: 'It has taken many to make me intelligent.' He
meant of course that he owed so much of his profound
perception of faith to those who loved, taught and influ-
enced him. So it is with respect to that curious relationship between the Bible and the Church.

In our century, as in most in the last two thousand
years, there have been Christian groups which have
thought that the Bible was all-sufficient to their thinking
about the faith, and that there was no need for a body of
church doctrine to be formed. In this they were wrong.
For because of our human wilfulness it is possible, and
has indeed been known, for the Bible to be (unintentionally or deliberately) misinterpreted, misused, misapplied
– and so falsified. There have been groups throughout our
century, as in the past, which have claimed to be Biblical
in their theology, and yet deny not only the doctrine of the
Trinity, but even that Christ is God. Studying the Bible
without reference to the developing teaching of the
Church leaves us at the mercy of our subjectivity, and in
danger, albeit unintentionally, of heresy. We who hand on
to you that which we ourselves received from our predecessors in the Church, and have made freshly our own,
have known how vital it has been, in the issues of our
times concerning religious belief, to have tested those

issues by the tradition of the Church through history and by the mind of the Church in the present.

Perhaps in our late twentieth century, with its Western insistence on the autonomy of the individual, we are peculiarly aware of the dangers of heresy as a potential watering down of the faith in a way which may not be as crucial for you who are to come. Yet this risk of vapid or idiosyncratic disparate 'theologies' is no new one. Indeed, there is New Testament evidence that the first Christians found it necessary to formulate church doctrine in order to defend the essentials of Christian truth. As the faith spread and the Church moved on in time and space, it is clear there were always doctrinal truths to be secured from new challenges to them. In the early days, you will recollect, the Church had to face opposition from Jews who denied that Jesus was the Messiah of God, and Greeks who could not countenance a doctrine of divine incarnation. And so I suppose it was inevitable that some quasi-Christian groups, affected by these arguments, would produce their own brand of teaching: the Docetics, for instance (from the root 'appear' or 'seem'), who claimed that, as God's Son, Jesus did not really appear in the flesh, but only seemed to; and the Gnostics (the root means 'know'), for whom mystical knowledge was the key to salvation, and whose version of the Christian faith, conflated with pagan ideas, was claimed by them to be a superior means of relating to God. So it was essential for the Church to form its theology in order to combat heresies from within, as well as attacks from without. We find plenty of evidence of this in the New Testament, for example in Paul's letter to the Colossians and in 1 John.

But there is another and richer reason for testing doctrine by the Church's teaching – one that is neither defensive nor conserving in its thrust. That is, from the earliest times we as Christians have wanted to possess the wealth of our inheritance, even as I yearn that you too should know those riches. As the growing Christian Church studied Scripture and saw the way Christ fulfilled the Old Testament; as it interpreted the New Testament in the light of its own day; so theology emerged as a living tradition in that Church. And so it remains and develops, excitingly alive, each age of the Church discovering more of those riches of its inheritance. Some of the riches we have found in our day I shall be sharing with you in later Letters. Sufficient for now to insist, as a part of that which we have reaffirmed in the experience of our own Christian life, on the importance and impact of that living doctrine formed by the Church through the ages. Tempting though it may seem to start all over again in order to stand over against a 'corrupt' Church, the effect in the end would be to cast away the rich truths the Church has been given. The very Bible itself, for instance, has come down to us through the Church of God, not least through those centuries in which faithful monks through the 'Dark Ages' treasured and preserved the very same Scriptures that all churches now enjoy.

Therefore, my dear fellow Christians of the future, do not be tempted to ignore in the sophistication of the new knowledge which will certainly be yours, the legacy of truth which generations of the Church's saints, scholars, monks and ordinary Christians have handed on to us through the twenty centuries which separate your day from that of the New Testament.

However, in urging you to respect the intricate relationship of Bible to Church I would not wish to undermine the very foundational character of Holy Scripture. All church tradition is subservient to it. As Dr Richard McBrien, a prominent Roman Catholic theologian of my day, put it:

'Tradition is not a fact-factory. It cannot create biblical "evidence" out of whole cloth. If something is not in scripture, it is not in scripture. And if it is not in scripture, it is not part of the deposit of faith. An appeal to tradition cannot make it so.' These are words to heed in relation to the scriptures which are foundational to the Church's teaching.

Related to our culture

In my many journeys around the Communion I serve I have understood more deeply the importance of relating faith to the culture we belong to. I think, for example, of the success and failure of Christian mission in Papua New Guinea, which was where my very first overseas trip took me. I noted the difference between those churches which used appropriate forms of native culture in liturgy as against those that imported the culture of the missionaries. I was delighted to see Anglican missionaries allowing tribal dances, employing terms, idioms and images from the culture around to bring the gospel alive. I recall, for example, entering a church dressed as usual in cope and mitre, escorted by two pretty, topless young girls in tribal dress, with bones through their noses! A far cry from Canterbury Cathedral, I remember thinking at the time!

That is but a local manifestation of what the Church has attempted to do through the centuries. It is called to relate its understanding of its faith to the world around it. In the early Church of the second century, teachers like Justin, for instance, drew with great skill upon current terms in order to translate for their age the unique event of God sending his Son into the world to save. He, like successive theologians down the ages, including many in this century from which I write, saw that Christians must use the language, concepts and thought forms available, to express and explore and sound in their own day the meaning of the 'faith once delivered to the saints'. It has to be done in every age because since faith is not only a relational experience but a holistic one, involving mind and imagination, thought as well as emotion, it must be expressed not only in all the many languages of worship and love, but in the language of human propositions. And in any age that propositional language can only approximate to the truth we are anxious to ponder and proclaim. So every age must wrestle again – as you must, as we have – with the way in which this age can express its appropriation of the ever-living Christ.

You will observe the problems with this immediately. First, there are the problems the translator faces. How can he or she be sure that the idea he or she wishes to convey in, say, Inuktitut (Eskimo language) is what Paul actually meant? (They have several tens of words for snow, but very few for fiery mountains.) Your translators, like ours, will tell you that whatever the subtlety of the computers available, catching the nuances faithfully of an idea or story is a matter of extraordinarily fine judgement. We are back to the necessities of the work of hermeneutics.

And that takes us into the profounder dimensions of the problem. For it is not only that this necessary use of current language becomes a filter through which we draw the essence of the gospel, possibly distorting or diminishing it in the process. It is also that having discerned this as true of our own engagement with faith statements, we recognise that the same cultural filtering and shaping must have occurred while the classic formulations of doctrine were being achieved. They too are anchored in the language and conceptual world in which they were coined. Take the formulation of 'God in Three Persons', which became the doctrine of the Trinity in the late fourth century. It was an authoritative theological statement of one of the profound mysteries of our faith, opening up riches of doctrinal perception for the ages to come, all of which have successively recognised its truth and explored it. Yet few scholars would deny that the argument behind it is rooted in concepts derived from fourth-century Greek culture and philosophy, much of it deeply alien to our thought today, and probably even more so to your thought tomorrow.

Let me give you an illustration of the complexities of handling Scripture faithfully. My generation is finding it very difficult to find an answer to the issue of divorce and remarriage and, it has to be confessed, the churches are not united in their response. In North America divorce has become so commonplace that one divorce for every two marriages is widely reported. England is only marginally better, with one in three marriages ending in divorce, but statistics indicate that we are rapidly catching up with the United States. The pain, distress and bitterness caused to families, especially children, by divorce, cast their shadows across communities and indeed churches too. But, as I have indicated, the churches are very sadly divided, with some strongly opposed to divorce in any shape or form, while others make room for remarriage. But how can the churches be so divided when the teaching of Scripture is said to be clear? Let us look briefly at the problem both Biblically and theologically.

First, there are five passages of Scripture in the New Testament (Mark 10:2–12; Matthew 5:31–32; 19:3–12; Luke 16:18; 1 Corinthians 7:10–16) where the issue is explicitly addressed. Each affirms marriage as a permanently binding commitment in which man and woman become one flesh. This fact dominates each passage and must be kept in mind. Jesus clearly saw a faithful, monogamous marriage as central to God's ideal for humanity. 'What God has joined together, let not man divide.'

However, on reading the texts we see that while there is that deep unity regarding the sanctity of marriage, there are also substantial differences which affect interpretation. Mark's reading which is primary is very severe. Divorce is forbidden and there are no grounds for separation. Full stop. The version in Matthew, however, differs in making adultery an 'exception', although Matthew 5:31–32 adds one significant element, that a divorced person, except one who has divorced on the grounds of adultery, if remarried, causes his new wife, though innocent, to be an adulteress. The Lukan passage is close to Mark's by disallowing divorce or remarriage. Finally, in 1 Corinthians we have the only passage which directly addresses an actual pastoral issue. It would appear that several Christian women in the mainly Gentile congregation of Corinth were married to unsympathetic unbelievers and they were wondering whether they had any right (or duty) to dissolve their marriages as a sign of their new freedom in Christ. Paul's reaction is pastoral and definite: marriage is for life and even if a Christian is married to an unbeliever, that does not constitute grounds for divorce. Indeed, the non-Christian is 'made holy' through the marriage bond. But then Paul says, surprisingly, 'But if the unbeliever leaves, let him do so. A believing man or woman is not bound in such circumstances' (7:15). Does this mean that the believer is now free to remarry? This question is not addressed, although in the context, Paul's preference for celibacy – in the light of the nearness of the second coming of Christ which he expected – might suggest that his advice would be: 'Remain as you are, single.' Nevertheless, according to many commentators, Paul is making room for remarriage in this circumstance.

Thus, the question for my generation is: How do we remain faithful to Scripture and the teaching of the Church in the light of these complexities and difficulties? There are those who will argue that Jesus' teaching is very clear and we should not depart from it. Others will argue that already in the first century it wasn't clear-cut: Matthew allows for divorce on the grounds of adultery and does not eliminate the possibility of remarriage thereafter; St Paul also seems to allow an exception if an 'unbeliever' separates from his wife. Today, we might question whether physical violence towards a spouse, or cruelty towards children in a marriage, might constitute a circumstance that would demand marital separation. And, again, we have to ask if in our culture (one quite different from that of the first century) the life-transforming gospel of Jesus Christ which 'makes all things new' might challenge our legalisms and offer fresh hope to those who, through no fault of their own, have the terrible experience of a failed marriage.

It is not my intention to offer a solution to our dilemma although, my dear friends of the future, I hope sincerely for your generation that your churches have a more united witness on this problem. All I have done is to outline the problem of interpretation. So, as the honest student of Scripture attempts to apply the Bible's teaching, there are at least three problems to address. First, there is the Biblical witness: What is it saying and is its witness univocal? That is to say, does it speak with one unambiguous voice? There follows the hermeneutical question: Are the Biblical writers actually confronting the same, or nearly the same, issue we are addressing? If not, we must be very careful in the conclusions we draw. There is finally the issue of culture which swirls around us and makes us ask: How can we be careful not to be sucked into a cultural relativism which makes us all dance to the tune of the world around us?

All this leads us straight to the most challenging of questions (remember how I said theology must confront uncertainties?): Can we ever be sure about any doctrine? How adequate is it as an expression of this part of our faith? And now we are at the heart of the controversies we have lived among in this century concerning belief. How have we engaged with them?

'Propositional' theology and 'personal' theology

Our varied approaches in handling these 'belief' controversies may perhaps be best understood by reference to two major styles of theology, which are important, I think, more for the attitude to doctrine each has epitomised than for inarguable conclusions reached by either. The traditional way of formulating doctrine is that of 'propositional theology'. It rests on the conviction that truth about God can, and indeed must, be expressed accurately (infallibly?) in human propositions which have been crystallised through the engagement together of the Church's best theological minds under the direction of the Holy Spirit. For some people, the validity of such propositional theology is assured through the teaching of the Church, set forth in those doctrines taught by the Church through the ages which supplies their authority (*autoritas*). Others, however, believe that revelation and Holy Scripture are synonymous. Such is the identification between God's Word made manifest in Jesus and his 'words' and those of others about him, that the Word is revealed in Holy Scripture and offers to the believer doctrines which can be known propositionally and accepted as authoritative.

However, in the modern period a more personal approach has appeared which, instead of focusing the issue on the objectivity of revelation through the Church's authoritative teaching or through the infallible words of Scripture, has sought to show that God's truth is revealed to individuals through encounter with a personal God. Basic to this approach is a perception that the divine mystery so defies our understanding that it is beyond explicit verbal formulation. God is the God who 'acts' and it is through reflection on his great works that the formulation of faith emerges. So, doctrines are the verbal crystallisations of a common experience of some aspect of God's nature, widely attested within the Church. William Temple put it in the following form: 'There are no revealed truths, only truths of revelation.' Our Doctrine Commission of 1976 was saying much the same when in its Report on 'Christian Believing' it stated: 'Theology is a process of reflection on faith that arises from revelatory experience; it is not the locus of revelation.'

Some reflections on these different approaches

I do apologise, dear friends, if all this seems rather remote from the real concerns of faith, but I assure you that it is not. You see, if the foundations of faith are not secure, no substantial building of faith can be erected. That is why I am labouring this point. But let us return to these different ways of determining and expressing belief, each of which in its own way has much to commend it, although there are flaws and difficulties with them all.

Let's take the first. For one thing, the very history of the Church in its struggle to formulate belief (to which struggles my generation has certainly added its own quota!)

suggests that at times truth and error have been difficult
if not impossible to distinguish. The 'authority' of the
Church's history has to be seen as to some extent ambiguous, when its living texture is a compound of such blood
and tears in the service of a truth only hindsight has sometimes clarified. And the claim for Scriptural authority for
doctrines looks equally ambiguous when the claimed
'perspicacity' of the Bible is seen in relation to Biblical criticism: how can we be sure of a doctrine if Scripture avow-
edly does not speak with one voice? Does such a
'propositional' approach imply a quantifiable view of
truth and error such that error can be excluded from the
Church like a draught kept out of a church building by a
draught excluder? Can this be valid?

And yet, and yet, as I have pointed out earlier, we can
understand this desire for clear, agreed statements of
belief, for we fear the destructive or vitiating power of
'error', which, full-blown, the Church has known as
'heresy'. It is this concern to keep the fullness of the gospel
in all its power, to be enjoyed and gloried in, in each successive age which lies behind all propositional theology.

The more 'personal' approach has its problems too. If
we deny that God has spoken authoritatively – through
the writings of St Paul, say – what value do we give his
teaching? Is it simply on a par with 'my' encounter with
God or the conversion experience of any Christian? When
Paul gives us sublime teaching about the church in
Ephesians do we regard that as normative for all
Christians everywhere or simply relative to his time? We
recognise, of course, that it is the freedom of understanding under the guidance of the Holy Spirit, and the
call to ever new experiencing of God's grace in every age,
which those approaching doctrine through a 'personal'
theology are attempting to secure. But to leave it undis-

tilled, unclarified, not 'received' by the Church as a whole and so not feeding into its organic life, is to let that potential doctrinal vitality trickle in a thousand streams away into the sand.

A synthesis

From the above it will be clear that I am seized by truths I find in both approaches. I have become convinced over the years that our best way of engaging with the uncertainties of which I have spoken is by putting both to service, not in a dialectic but in a continuum.

For the strength of the 'personal' approach is that the root of every doctrine must be that which comes first – our experience of Christ. As when the Church began: he met the disciples and they found faith not in his arguments ultimately – though never man spoke like this man – but in him. What they experienced, and what the early Church experienced through direct contact with them through the first fifty years of the Church's life, was to become the foundation of Christian doctrine. (Astronomers have told us – you in your century may know much more about it now – that the whole evolution of our planet was determined in the first three seconds of its creation. Something of that same truth holds good for our faith. The whole of potential Christian thought was immanent in the explosive new reality which was the intervention in our lives of God, through Christ and the gift of the Holy Spirit.)

Revelation, then, to the Church corporate and to each individual should, will, always be in its truth deeply personal. But it must not halt there; it must never halt there. Otherwise that testing which makes it a gift to the whole Church will not take place. The early formulations by the early Church, elements of which appear in the Gospels

and Epistles, and indeed the Gospels and Epistles themselves, all show the felt necessity of a process from the
personal to the propositional: 'I write these things to you
who believe in the name of the Son of God so that you
may know that you have eternal life' (1 John 5:13). And
Paul, who speaks in Galatians 1 of his experience of direct,
personal revelation – 'I want you to know, brothers, that
the gospel I preached is not something that man made up.
I did not receive it from any man, nor was I taught it;
rather, I received it by revelation from Jesus Christ' – this
same Paul of personal revelation probed the doctrine
inherent in it, formulated it and taught it with that profundity which has, through the propositional process,
helped the Church through the ages not only to know
Whom she has believed, but Who he is, and what is his
relationship with us.

So we have found it right to hold on to this simple and
important truth, which we offer to you of the future as
tested in our own experience: that theology, and the doctrine that flows from it, is the work of Christian men and
women, in the context of the Church, as they seek to
reflect on their own experience of Christ and how God has
addressed them and the Church in their age through him;
as they seek to understand and describe the significance
of the wonder of God becoming one with us, and
'propose' to their world, in the language their world
speaks, the mystery of God's grace.

Relevant to living

The final thing we should observe about our theology, our
formulating of our belief, is that it must have practical
consequences. This is an enormous area which we in this
century have spent much time and energy both ponder-

ing and acting on. Our churches have recognised the implication of our faith for our service in society, though sometimes laggardly and sometimes hesitantly. The glory of such recognition shone through the Confessing Church in Nazi Germany, memorably expressed by Dietrich Bonhoeffer, not only in words but by his living and dying. I am sure he will be a Christian hero in your time as in ours. His willingness to face even death for the sake of justice and truth is an inspiring example of courage and faith. My century has been a century of martyrs; men and women have faced the life implications of their believing.

For Christian doctrine is not head knowledge only. To say, for example, that 'Jesus is Lord' is far more searching in its consequences not just for my lifestyle but for my attitude of heart to life itself, than, say, a formula such as $E=MC^2$. The latter, like much knowledge, though it may have long-term consequences for the organisation of human life, does not affect my moral being. I can be an immoral person and still go with Einstein's theorem. But I cannot believe Jesus Christ is Lord, and let my immorality go unchallenged. Nor let public ill go unchallenged, or see public good put at risk. A theological statement like that is not of the same order as other forms of knowledge. Theology thus passes into discipleship, and from there into worship and service. Which is why all through our century our Church has been unpopular from time to time in different parts of the world with those in secular power who do not see that theology is life-challenging and life-changing. It is far, far more than a theoretical discipline. It is far, far more than the internal conversation of the Church. It travels from the head to the heart and then to the world in which we live. Or else it dies, for it has atrophied.

*

I have written at such length to you about how we have tested and probed these truths by which we have lived, so that you may share with us something of the journey we have made, as each age of the Church must make it. Out of it all have emerged those certainties to which we hold fast; they have been the constants on our journey, as we believe they will be yours. So, I hope you have been able to glimpse enough of our place in the world of Christian thought and struggle to be able now to share, in my next Letter, something of what to us is primary: what we have received, and found true for ourselves, of the mystery of the nature of God.

But before we go on to reflect together about that, I have to close down my computer and go to our General Synod in York where we shall be debating many topical issues, including the revision of our liturgies for the year 2000 and beyond. I know we all feel a sympathy with the cry of the great Father of the Church, St Basil of Caesarea, who once said: 'Synods I salute from afar!' And yet I value these times when the representatives of the Church, lay as well as clergy, get together to guide the Church forward, so that we hand over to you, my dear friends, a Church in good heart, sound in doctrine and organisation.

Yours, in the excitement and hope of discovering God's truth,

LETTER 2

The Creator God

Dear Friends of the Future,

The meeting of our General Synod turned out to be fruitful and positive. It was held together with some interesting debates spiced with gentle humour and all in a good Christian spirit. (I wonder if the Anglicans among you have a General Synod in your day and, if so, what form it takes.) We had a 'lively' discussion (that's very nearly a euphemism!) about liturgical revision. There was a moment in the debate which underlined the relevance of my comments to you in my last Letter about how we apply Scripture. For I was struck by the attitudes of two speakers who, from opposite positions on liturgy, were each quite sure that they had the truth. Both were 'absolutists'. The first, arguing from tradition, took the view that no other liturgy than *The Book of Common Prayer* was either necessary or helpful; no departure from what was a sacred text was allowable. The other, wholly deaf to such an approach, was equally forcefully convinced that the past had nothing to share with us; we had to start from scratch!

As I listened to the debate I got to pondering what, if any, changes might be suggested even in the wording of the Creed, and, in particular, in its magnificent opening statements about the Creator God. And it struck me, while reflecting slightly mischievously on what proposals might emerge, that in those simple and profound opening declarations, and the questions they confront, we have a very good example of what I was talking about in my last Letter. I mean by this that the way we talk about God thoughtfully as Christians must always involve returning to the roots of our faith in the Bible, hearing what the Church has taught through the ages, taking part in our own culture's dialogue with that, and addressing the whole to the perennial questions of how humanity should live.

For, of course, the Creed itself was arrived at, and has been maintained in (more or less) its existing forms, precisely through the interaction of those four activities. And therefore when I want to declare to you who are to come what things we have found to be true and sustaining in our faith in this twentieth century, it is worth starting with what has been handed on to us through that process in the past, and sharing with you how we've experienced it in the present.

We shall begin, as Alice in Wonderland was famously told to do, at the beginning. The Creed, that known as the Nicene–Constantinople Creed, begins:

> We believe in one God
> the Father, the almighty,
> maker of heaven and earth,
> of all that is,
> seen and unseen.

Millions of us across the world together declare, Sunday by Sunday, even day by day, that this is the God we believe in: that he is the one and only deity, that his relationship with us is parental, that power is ultimately all his, and that everything that exists, observed or not yet discovered, he made.

So the tradition of the Church, what it has taught through the ages, begins exactly where the Bible begins – with God the Initiator of it all – and expands on that as the rest of the Bible does into the story of God's parenting of us, the story of his single sovereignty, the story of the absolute mightiness which lies behind not only the act of Creation but the wonder of his saving of that Creation, and the story of the interrelation with each other, through him, of heaven and earth.

Both Scripture and the traditional teaching of the Church, then, start from an all-important perception, that in the vital issue of existence itself, and the relationship of that existence to God, it is God who takes the initiative. 'In the beginning, God created' are the opening words of the Bible. He is the Creator who calls all things out of nothing into being. (He is also the Being who, having made things to 'be', offers them a sustaining loving care in a relationship with himself, for which the nearest word we can find is a parental one – 'Father'; and of that more anon.) The key truth we need to stay with for the moment is that it all starts from God: he has the authority and the dynamic of being the Source, not just of ourselves, but of all the universes that are.

You will see the vital implications of this. No matter what unimaginable discoveries lie ahead for us in these dying last years of our century, and for you in yours, those discoveries take us further into the marvel of God the Initiator. Rather than diminishing his awesomeness, they increase it. For he is not, and never has been, a 'God of the gaps', merely another name for the question mark over those (many) things we do not yet understand or know about the nature and extent of the universe, or even about our own Earth. Rather he is the God who fathers the unimaginable into existence. The more we learn of the nature of that existence, the more beyond our conceiving becomes the Being who could not only take the initiative so to create, but could sustain that initiative in the ongoing life of that Creation.

For that is the point of starting, as the Bible does, as the Church has done, as I have found I must, with the God who takes the initiative. If he is such a God, it follows that by his nature he continues to be an initiative-taker in relation to his Creation, ourselves included. (We need to note that when we talk about people being initiative-takers, or people of initiative, we are speaking of a consistent quality in their character, not a one-off action. And so it is with God.) Therefore we may expect of him continuing initiative; he goes on doing it. And will, unimaginably.

And, of course, that is just what the Bible describes in narrative after narrative, and what the Church's own experience of him has been in century after century, and what person after person has described from their own individual experience: that God takes the initiative, in the ongoing life of Creation as he did in its origin.

Now this conviction that God is a continuing initiator is vital in our current dialogue with our contemporary culture. I shall return in a moment to issues concerning Creation itself, and what their implications are for our world. But for the moment I want to take this truth of our God as an *ongoing initiator*, and lay it alongside the grieving agnosticism of our times. For perhaps one of the most powerful and accurate statements of our century's religious hopelessness, made almost exactly at its halfway point, was about an apparent lack of ongoing divine initiative. It was written by an Irishman in French, and translated into English. I wonder whether it's still on your library shelves, and performed by (what I hope remain) fine live theatre companies. Samuel Beckett's *Waiting for Godot*, seen by us as a classic to be revived at regular intervals, is still a devastating account of faith lost and grieved over, even though its existentialist context has largely gone. In it there is a speech which has been widely quoted throughout the second half of our twentieth century, as summarising what many people of our times fear may be the truth about God's relationship with his Creation. Stripped of its verbal cul-de-sacs it reads like this:

> Given the existence . . . of a personal God . . . with white beard . . . outside time without extension, who from the heights of divine apathia . . . loves us dearly with some exceptions . . . and suffers . . . with those who for reasons unknown are plunged in torment . . . it is established beyond all doubt . . . that as a result of the labours left unfinished . . . it is established what many deny . . . that man in short that man in brief . . . is seen to waste and pine waste and pine . . . to shrink and dwindle . . . to shrink and dwindle . . . the facts are there . . . alas alas . . . the labours abandoned left unfinished . . . alas alas abandoned unfinished . . .

Now there is much here we might return to, but we need to start from this sense that the speech ends with: that 'the labours [are] abandoned, left unfinished'. For part of the point of starting our thinking about God by reflecting on him as Creator is precisely because it emphasises, in counter to this despairing view, that quality of his nature which takes all necessary initiatives. Therefore Creation itself in all its complexity, and humanity within it, far from being abandoned, is subject to the ongoing

creativity of God. And what that ongoing divine initia-
tive-taking, divine creativity, means, we can begin to
understand when we look at what is implied in the claim
that he is 'maker . . . of all that is, seen and unseen'.

God as Creator

'In the beginning God (*Elohim*) created the heavens and
the earth.' With these words the story begins of the most
profound relationship – that between God and the human
race. It is a relationship, the story tells us, initiated by
God. What are the vital elements of that relationship as
humanity has come to know it, the Bible has recorded it,
and his people through the ages have experienced it?

(i) The word used of God here – *Elohim* – marks the first
essential element. It is the most general and least specific
of all names for God in the Old Testament, coming from a
root meaning 'very great or very strong'. And that
concept of inconceivable strength and power sums up
how ancient Hebrews saw their Creator. The kind of
majestic power inherent in creating the universe is what
humanity first responds to in God. Our Creeds retain the
priority of this in their use of the adjective 'Almighty' to
describe how we first think about God. So the majestic
opening chapter of Genesis is chronicling, as a basis of all
that is to come, humanity's awed recognition that it is in
relationship with a Being of inconceivable power.

It is important that we do not lose our grasp on this
earliest human awareness, in the developing understanding that was – and is – to come. For the extraordinary magnanimity of God's relationship with us can only
be kept in focus if we retain a sense of wonder at his
mightiness. And that same mightiness we are going to
experience again and again as the story unfolds of his

relationship with us: most powerfully – and also most mysteriously – in his defeat, through the resurrection of Jesus Christ from the dead, of how death destroys us. It is precisely the same order of power, might, at work in that dismantling of the destructiveness of death, as was at work in the creating of the universe with which the Bible begins the story of the relationship.

(ii) I used the word 'mysteriously' a moment ago. And that's the second vital element in the story of our relationship with God. Not just a marvelling at an overwhelming power, but an awed wonder at something, Someone, who is mysterious, transcendent, the nature and style of whose acts of power speak of something not merely mightier than myself but of a quite different order of being. What we see of God in his Creation work disarms our arrogance, puts our hubris into perspective; the night sky, for instance:

> When I consider your heavens,
>   the work of your fingers,
> the moon and the stars,
>   which you have set in place,
> what is man that you are mindful of him,
>   or the son of man that you care for him?
> (Psalm 8:3–4)

John Keats was to say much the same for us, centuries later in another time and another country:

> When I behold upon the night's starred face
> Huge cloudy symbols of a high romance . . .
>
> On the brink of the world I stand alone and think
> Till love and fame to nothingness do sink.

This response of awe and wonder, this sense of the mysteriousness of it all, this sense of a Mind behind it which is beyond our grasp, is not simply that of primitive man in an early stage of humanity's journey. For rather than simplifying our basic questions, modern cosmological science has deepened the mystery. So we find ourselves asking questions which arise from a strong sense of wonder. Why doesn't the cosmos begin with chaos instead of a primal state of amazing order? Why are all the constants of nature there from the Big Bang on? Why do the same physical necessities obtain everywhere throughout the universe? Why is it that intelligibility itself seems to run like a refrain throughout the created order, making science itself possible? Here is a recent Astronomer Royal, Sir Arnold Wolfendale, speaking of the same mystery quite recently:

> There seems little doubt that a 'Big Bang' occurred some 13 billion years ago and that the universe has been evolving ever since. But what preceded the Big Bang, and how will the universe develop in the future? Will the universe cease to expand eventually and then start to contract again, resulting in a 'Big Crunch'?! If so, will it bounce, and start off again? Indeed, is this the best way of understanding the origin problem, to say that there was no origin, and that the universe has always been expanding and contracting in turn? What about the nature of time – does it always proceed smoothly in the same direction or, if and when the universe starts to collapse, does time reverse along with space? . . . All the problems listed above have, in my view, a religious component. Concerning the nature of a God responsible for all things, my own faith has strengthened with increased experience of the discoveries of science; it is, to me, unthinkable that the whole edifice has a purely mechanistic origin . . .

In other words, there is enough about the nature of things as we are discovering them to be, to make belief in God not wilful but still a serious and proper hypothesis. So that loss of the sense of transcendence experienced by so many in our age is not in fact inherent in the work of twentieth-century scientific enquiry. Quite the reverse. 'Through my scientific work,' writes Professor Paul Davies, self-confessedly not a 'conventional believer', 'I have come to believe more and more strongly that the physical universe is put together with an ingenuity so astonishing that I cannot accept it as brute fact. There must, it seems to me, be a deeper level of explanation.'

(iii) We have spoken of an almighty God putting out a creative power unimaginable but indicated by the Big Bang with which our universe began, and we have spoken of an awe-inspiring God, the nature and intricacy and mystery of whose design fills us with wonder and a sense of the transcendent, the beyond-our-imagining, the holy. Rightly reflected on, these two aspects of the kind of God he is make me tremble and fear him, and yet wonder at him and worship him with awe and humbleness. But the story of humanity's relationship with God as we first know him through his initial act of creation, is much profounder and more subtle than that. And the clue is in the kind of creation we find ourselves a part of. For God has not created mere artefacts, static and without life. Rather, he has created life itself. And the relationship of a creator with something that is alive is necessarily quite different from that of a creator with something that is but an object.

The old story of *Pygmalion* helps us to see what is implied. The carved figure of the woman is to be delighted in as beautiful. But when life is breathed into it, so that it takes on an identity of its own, then the relationship between this creature and its creator becomes much more subtle and demanding. George Bernard Shaw's version of it, and the musical that followed it, *My Fair*

Lady, both made the same point. (Do you still enjoy either of those, I wonder?) The relationship is not between a creator and an inanimate object; it has become a relationship between persons.

And so it is with the God we have learned to love. It is the fact that we can and do speak of him with awe and wonder and even a right sort of holy fear, and yet address him as Father, which is so distinctive of the Christian relationship with God. In other words, the divine act of Creation is seen as an event, albeit a profoundly significant one, in a larger story. Pictures from Genesis direct us towards this. Not only the delight of the Maker at each stage of this first event of the story – 'And God saw that it was good' – but the tender intimacy of that picture of God walking in the garden with Adam and Eve, which is surely meant to convey not only the Creator's delight in his world, but his capacity for sharing that delight with humanity, and the extremely personal relationship that implies. It is a relationship for which the Bible and the Church have used the term 'Father'.

And this 'parenting' relationship is one I shall return to again and again as I explore with you in these Letters what we have found to be trustworthy and true in the faith handed on to us. For it is the thread of understanding that leads us ever deeper into the nature of 'God-with-us'.

Humanity and the natural world

'And God saw that it was good.' We are coming more and more to recognise today that a part of that 'goodness' is in the right relationship between human beings and the world. This is where the culture I live in, and the Biblical account of Creation, engage with each other very powerfully. Indeed, if you in your generation are to enjoy the Earth and its wonder of species, then we need to learn both soon and deeply what it means that the Earth is God's creation, shared in delight with humanity.

For we have seen in the plundering of the world around us, for short-term profit or to serve a particular lifestyle of humanity at no matter what cost to the environment, one aspect of what can happen if God's role in the universe is not acknowledged. Two characteristic human attitudes to the natural world can ensue, and they have done so, devastatingly, in this century. One is to exploit the world's resources ruthlessly. The other is to 'worship' the natural world. This latter is harder to describe, because its effects are not so immediately obvious. It can sometimes be seen when a marked imbalance develops such that a human life is seen as less important than that of an animal, for instance. Or our anxiety about the despoliation of our countryside leads us to oppose all new buildings or roads, even where they are not a needless luxury but a necessity to a community. These are difficult and sensitive matters of judgement, and we are unlikely to get them right if we do not recognise the fundamental truth about the relationship between the natural order and ourselves.

That is, that God made it and delights in it with an exuberant joy over all manner of living things coming into being. Creation is therefore for God, and for humanity only under God. We are the pinnacle of God's Creation, but not its centre. Not everything in Creation is for us; non-human beings have their own God-given place in God's world.

Second, the kind of God he is, a good God, is fundamental to the kind of Creation he has made, and to right attitudes towards it. His mercy extends not just to humanity, but to everything he has created. There is a delightful

Rabbinic story based on Genesis which sums up a responsible Biblical attitude towards Creation:

> When God created Adam, he showed him all the trees of the Garden of Eden and said to him: 'See my works, how lovely they are, how fine they are! All I have created I created for you. Take care not to corrupt and destroy my universe, for if you destroy it, no-one will come after you to put it right.' (Ecclesiastes, Rabbah 7)

You will see, of course, how this conviction about a Creator God sets us right in those double environmental dangers which we have struggled with for so long, and which I pray your own generation will have vanquished. For to abandon understanding of our human role as but the servants of the God of Creation leads directly on the one hand to the dying out of thousands of species, together with the devastation of the earth's resources, and the excesses of nature worship on the other.

Some current problems

I reflect on that Rabbinic story. And I reflect on how, right through the Bible, humanity is shown as agent of God's care for the Earth, exercising responsible stewardship; from the famous Genesis command to Adam and Eve to 'be fruitful and increase in number; fill the earth and subdue it. Rule over the fish of the sea and the birds of the air and over every living creature that moves on the ground', to the tender words of Jesus about sparrows: 'Are not two sparrows sold for a penny? Yet not one of them will fall to the ground unperceived by your Father.'

These mark the twin poles of our proper human relationship with the natural order: on the one hand exercising authority in it, dominating it, subduing it; on the other, at the same time and by the same actions, tenderly aware of, and respectful of, its beauty, fragility and unique identity. So no plans we make or actions we take should be disregarding of either of those aspects of our right stance towards Creation and all that is in it.

Keeping those poles in balance because they are the way God created us to be amid our natural world, would enable us to approach both sensitively and effectively the three main issues which are currently pressing on us, and which, if we don't handle them better than we are doing at the moment, may well have helped to maim and disfigure the world that we hand on to you to whom I write. Forgive us that we have been so slow and reluctant to face these issues; forgive us especially for the price you will be paying for our lack of proper stewardship. There are three areas which I feel quite passionately we are failing in as God's stewards: (i) the exploitation of the world's resources; (ii) the pollution of the natural world on a global scale; and (iii) not controlling our over-population.

We are currently getting all these badly wrong because we will not keep in steady view both elements of our God-ordained stewardship – the respectful and tender as well as the dominating. So, though we pay lip-service to Dean Swift's famous edict about the best service we can do the world, we deny it by our actions: 'He gave it for his opinion, that whoever could make two ears of corn or two blades of grass to grow upon a spot of ground where only one grew before, would deserve better of mankind, and do more essential service to his country . . .'

For although our laboratories have achieved technical marvels in assisting agriculture to develop strains of grain, and grass resistant to disease and much more fruitful, the materialist pressures in this same culture have been decimating the rain forests. They are disappearing from the face of the Earth at the rate of 1.5 acres per second night and day; and there are global consequences of this in the wholesale destruction of delicate ecological balances we simply have not been prepared seriously to face. The same applies to issues of pollution. The human race is filthying its world by belching into the atmosphere every year several billion tons of carbon, mainly from burning fossil fuels; mainly, that is, from maintaining a lifestyle which is inappropriate to the natural resources given us in the world. And that same reckless refusal to respect the realities of what the Earth can support has led us to a very grave risk of over-population. In 1945 the world population was 1.2 billion; in 1992, 5.5 billion. Our present projections are 9 billion persons by 2032. That is your generation, to whom I write, and your world. Shall we have acted in time, by responsible stewardship of our families, to save over two thirds of your world from living in desperate, indeed absolute, poverty? Shall we have recognised that part of our God-given relationship to our world is so to control our own numbers, by family planning in its many forms, that we do not behave like human locusts on its surface, eating up the seed-corn which should be your inheritance, you who are to come? I do not know (although you will). I only know that no occupant of Augustine's chair ever had greater cause to speak sternly and directly of the consequences of denying, in the way we live, the ordinances of God, than I have today. Direct and appalling results will follow if we do not take seriously, with urgency, the mandate of God in respect of our relationship to the natural order of things, and so correct our offence against the good Earth towards which we should be the agents of God's care.

I am able to speak so stern a warning and yet be a voice of hope, not despair, because there is one all-important way in which the Christian perspective on all this differs from that of the secular voices which are also uttering warnings. That is, we live in the Christian conviction that this life is not the end; that the Earth will be renewed, becoming, with heaven, in the profound mystery of God's dealings with us, 'a new heaven and a new earth'. I do most firmly believe that we are called to co-operate with God in his care for the world. And, indeed, it may be that in some mysterious way our achieving these balances will contribute to whatever that unimaginable re-creation may be.

But I also believe that when we battle to establish right ways of engaging with our environment, we can do so in both hope and trust; hope in the good purposes of God, and trust in that tender care which, along with his might and authority over us, marks his divine relationship not just with the world he has created, but with the human race which, the Bible assures us, and our own experience confirms, he joys over and delights in. 'So do not be afraid; you are of more value than many sparrows...'

And it is the special, personal nature of that which I want to write to you about in my next Letter.

Yours in the security of God's creating love,

LETTER 3

Discovering God as Father

Dear Friends of the Future,

'You are of more value than many sparrows . . .' As I write to you it is Spring, and there is a quarrel of sparrows outside my study window here at Lambeth. The gardens are just putting on their first fragile green after a long and hard Winter. I could have no more significant wish for you who are to come than the hope that still, in the face of the environmental concerns of my last Letter, this miracle of new life speaks to you as it does to us, of the sustaining of God. And of something much more. For the God of that new life is that same God who chose to place himself in a love-bond, not only with his Creation at large, but specially and uniquely with humanity. So as I look out through this window, I do not only see a 'created order' fulfilling the will of God. Far more marvellously, I, a mere part of that created order, am at this moment able to *talk with him directly*. Talk not only in praise of the wonder of what I am seeing, but also in dialogue about my own place in it, about our own human responsibilities for it, and above all about his purposes, for all of us both within it and beyond it. In other words I, in my human-ness, am able to respond to God as 'Person'.

And it is of those wonders – and mysteries – of God as Person that I want to write to you today. For of all the truths that have kept us through the hard years of this century, and indeed sustained the long line of those who preceded me in the chair of Augustine, perhaps this is the one that matters most; the one that I long should be real for you of my grandchildren's generation, and for those who follow you. For it is out of the relationship, Person with persons, between God and his most precious creation, the human race, that the wonderful story comes. The story whose truths I so want to hand on to you, with all that we in our generation have discovered in them. I touched on this in my last Letter to you, but now I want to focus on it.

I am spending no time here on the question of whether there actually is a God. Not because I am not aware that for many people, no doubt in your century as in mine, that remains an open question. But, as John Habgood, former Archbishop of York, colleague for a number of years and brilliant apologist for the faith, once said reflectively after attending a public debate on 'Does God exist?' immediately after spending three days on a Lenten Retreat, 'It is very hard to rehearse arguments for the existence of God when you have just spent three days intensely in his presence!' Just so, these Letters to you are not theological arguments for the existence of God, but descriptions of how I have experienced him in the world as well as in my own life, and about what kind of map the Bible and the Church have given me to find my way round that experience. And about what its implications are for our life together. It is in the Bible, the foundation document of my faith, that right at the very beginning the first hint is to be found of the special way in which God is to be known to and by humanity in the context of the created world.

For the first hint of the special, indeed unique, relationship between human beings and their Creator, as the Bible describes it, appears in the first chapter of Genesis. There the story-teller speaks of God's purpose to 'make man in our image, in our likeness' (Genesis 1:26). And from then on the entire story of the Bible, from this point to its climax in the book of Revelation, has at its core that special relationship between God and humanity. And so it introduces us to a God who is not only 'All-mighty', and 'mysterious' in his creating, but one who is personal in his relationship with human beings because he has made them uniquely like him.

A 'personal' God. One clue is that the Bible speaks about God primarily in a series of stories rather than in a series of propositions, so that from the first we experience him as the 'Person' at their centre rather than the 'idea' in an argument. The Creation stories describe a universe whose basic features of beauty and goodness are qualities we recognise in the beautiful and complex ecology we observe around us. But far more vivid than any theoretical 'idea' of a God we might extrapolate from that, or even that the Bible develops in statements or arguments from that, is the series of stories about humankind dramatically engaged with that same God in this world he has made. A God who is continually involving us with him, Person with persons, in the action. So in the Bible narrative we get glimpses of him in converse with his people, in action or reaction, in anger or in tenderness, indicating plan and promise or warning and even threat. Biblically we may not avoid thinking about God as Person.

So that claim about humanity being made 'in the like-ness' of God emphasises a family relationship between God and humankind. From the outset humanity is envis-aged as being on very personal and intimate terms with the Deity. And descriptions of him as 'seeing', 'hearing', 'speaking', becoming 'angry', are projected onto him to convey the Almighty's nearness to his people. Such descriptions are of course in one sense anthropo-morphisms, because they describe the transcendent God in terms properly only applicable to human beings. So in absolute terms they are nowhere near accurate – just as your scribbled outline 'drawing', at two years old, of your mother, was nowhere near accurate. But in another sense they have validity, for the Biblical insistence on God's per-sonhood is vital to our knowledge of him; and our only guess at what might be meant by divine personhood is its analogy, which the Bible insists on, with human person-hood. That is, we read back from the notion of humanity 'made in God's image' a way of perceiving God by describing him in terms applicable to human personality, while recognising that these are mere approximations, a sort of theological algebraic use of terms to indicate that which cannot be set out in fullness.

The two-way dialogue

What are the essentials of God as Person? Vitally, since persons show themselves through relationship, the Bible insists that he both addresses us and is addressed by us – he hears us. He is neither silent nor deaf: indeed, when he appears to be deaf his people cry out to him to be true to his nature and hear them. He is a God who acts, but this action is frequently related in the Bible to the dialogue, the exchange, between God and his people. The Psalms, for instance, are full of this two-way dialogue, in which the psalmist speaks directly to God of his need or distress or delight or hope, and 'hears' God's response in the depth of his own heart, or in the circumstances around him:

> Hear, O LORD, and answer me,
>> for I am poor and needy.
> Guard my life, for I am devoted to you.
>> You are my God; save your servant
> who trusts in you.
>
> (Psalm 86:1–2)

> In the day of my trouble I will call to you,
>> for you will answer me.
>
> (Psalm 86:7)

Moses is described as taking this person-to-person dialogue with God into an intimacy rarely experienced. He stands out in Israel's history because of this intimacy with God: 'Since then, no prophet has risen in Israel like Moses, whom the Lord knew face to face' (Deuteronomy 34:10).

Yet this intimate dialogue continues in the New Testament, beginning with Christ's own dialogue with his Father while among us sharing our humanity, and continuing into the history of the Church of which we are a part. Here the way God is to be understood as Person through relationship achieves one of the deepest of bonds – that of parent. Christ uses the intimacy of child to parent. He speaks to him as 'Father'. For those to whom the 'maleness' of this creates a difficulty, or for whom the notion of 'father' has been permanently spoiled through ill-usage, it is vital to hold on to the key relationship – that of parent; loving, strong, gentle parent. So Jesus talks to God as he wants *us* to talk to God, as to one who loves us and shares his purposes with us.

Indeed, to pray to God as 'Abba', as Jesus did, is to embark on a relationship which is fundamental to the Christian life. It is a debatable point whether or not Jesus was the first to call God 'Abba' (Luke 11:1–4). Some scholars are confident that no one before Jesus had the temerity to do so. Others claim that the fact that the Old Testament speaks of God as Father intimates that individuals would most likely have done so. Whatever the truth of this, we can be sure that the passage illustrates Jesus' own relationship with God. He saw God as his father and parent, who loved and cared for him as intimately and as closely as we who are parents care for those we love.

Sharing the parent's purposes

This sense of God's personal, parental relationship with us being such that we are one with his purposes comes through again and again, both in the story the Bible tells, and what our Church's history shows, of our dialogue with him. I have found it in my own life too, as well as in the life of the people of God in my day. And I am quite certain that the years between you and me will have told the same story.

So, for instance, St Paul, both in describing his dialogue with God about his personal needs, and in his vision of God's great cosmic design in which we share a role, speaks of the purposes of God which are being unfolded to us, and in which our role is of crucial significance. He tells of his pleading with God to be relieved of his 'thorn in the flesh' which seemed 'a messenger of Satan, to torment me'. Three times, he tells us, he 'pleaded with the Lord to take it away from me'. God's reply is, 'My grace is sufficient for you, for my power is made perfect in weakness' (2 Corinthians 12:7b–9). The point is that God's denial in this dialogue is not gratuitous but purposeful: Paul is to achieve, mysteriously, a greater power through it.

I have always found this passage a great help to me in understanding the mystery of prayer. We sometimes struggle with the fact that life is not always fair. Evil often seems to triumph over goodness, and prayer may seem so feeble at times. I recall a former student of mine who went to work as a missionary teacher in Zimbabwe and was killed in a pointless murder. Only a young man, he had so much to offer. A young widow and two small children were left to grieve his death. Where is God when terrible things like that happen, we ask ourselves? At such times we shall get it all wrong if we leave out of the equation God's remarkable power to transform what may seem to us to be beyond hope. 'My power is made perfect in weakness.' Paul's testimony is that of the Church's in history. God in Christ is able to fan the ashes of our despair and disappointment to bring new fires of hope and blessing.

Paul's dialogue of questioning God's purposes in his personal ministry is all part of his dialogue with God concerning the whole of Creation. He speaks of the entire cosmos, which 'waits in eager expectation for the sons of God to be revealed', and which 'itself will be liberated from its bondage to decay'. That is, the special relationship with the human race which is worked at and gradually discerned in this dialogue with God is at the heart of God's great purpose of redeeming Creation: 'In all things God works for the good of those who love him, who have been called according to his purpose' (Romans 8:19, 21, 28). So God and humankind talk together about that gradually unfolding plan for the fullness of time (Ephesians 1:10) in which we are God's partners.

Here, it seems to me, God as Person, known in dialogue and act, speaks directly to our culture; certainly to the cynicisms and near despair of the culture I live in. I write from a post-modernist world, where the claim is that none of the 'meta-narratives' or 'superstories' by which humanity has lived in the past hold good for us any more; the *grands récits* are concluded. Even the ultimate faith claim, that of Science, to have access to truth, is now greeted by much of the West with some disillusionment and suspicion. Paul Davies and John Gribbin wrote recently in what they called *The Matter Myth: Towards 21st Century Science* that the 'new physics', relativity theory, quantum theory, chaos theory – all of which will have been superseded by your time at the rate things are going – even these stumbling steps have blown apart the scientific materialism of the past with its comparatively closed system. As a review by Arthur Jones in *The Third Way* puts it:

> Matter has been deposed, to be replaced by concepts such as organisation, complexity and information. Mystery has returned, as scientists develop theories that take us way beyond common sense, indeed to a reality that is impossible to visualise. And further, the horrors of modern warfare, environmental damage and global pollution are now often blamed on science . . . Try as they may, scientists cannot wash their hands of all responsibility; [for] detailed work on the history and philosophy of science, and more recently the sociology of knowledge, have shown that science's claim to be uniquely objective cannot be upheld.

So, the cultural world I live in is a cold and lonely one, which sees each of us as on our own in a hostile and indifferent universe, with no convincing overarching story, not even that of science, to give us meaning. At best, there is a spiritual market-place in which each of us is required to select the psychic bargain of our choice. At worst, the view would be that there are no such bargains, for all of them are rubbish, detritus from the lumber rooms of our spiritual history; a kind of spiritual 'boot sale' where ultimately all is junk. (I wonder if boot sales have continued into your time. They are immensely popular right now, indeed a sort of subculture.) Such a view makes nonsense of any human claim to an ultimate meaning for its existence.

And over against this stands the Christian experience of the God who is Person, who is in dialogue with his Creation, humanity, and who involves that humanity in the largeness and goodness of his purposes. The God of whom the Bible speaks, to whom the Church in her history attests, and through whom countless individuals have found and do find meaning and purpose – this is the God I affirm to you as in our experience standing over against all the negativities and vapidities of our relativistic age.

As most surely he will in yours. For his 'dialogue with a purpose' is recorded as continuing right down through the history of the Christian Church. As I write to you now my mind flashes to two former Archbishops of Canterbury whose ministries cannot be separated from their dialogue with God. The first will be known to you, Thomas Cranmer, who wrote the peerless *Book of Common Prayer* in Lambeth Palace in a room just a few yards from the Chapel where I pray daily. Thomas, a scholarly man, was also a man of peace. He had the misfortune to live at a time in English history where to be a man of principle could easily take one to the scaffold. Thomas Cranmer knew what it was to waver even in the strength of faith. Convinced though he was of the truth of Reformation faith he recanted three times before his terrible death. And then, perhaps realising that he could not die betraying his convictions, he denied the recantations he had written, and upon arriving at the burning pyre thrust his hand into the flames crying: 'This hand has sinned.' I am often moved by that story because of the terrible loneliness of his last journey. Our Church exists today because of the faith of people like this. There is something deeply reassuring about the frailty of that great man's faith. He knew what it was to waver when confronted by the instinct for self-preservation. Yet he also knew the tender grace of his Lord when he needed strengthening.

Another great but lesser-known archbishop I admire is Archibald Tait, who entered into this office towards the end of the last century. Before becoming a bishop Archibald was Dean of Carlisle. He was blessed, as I am, by having a devoted and loving wife as companion. But tragedy struck them when in the space of five weeks their five little daughters died of scarlet fever. I look back from my times on their times and wonder how it is humanly possible to carry on when your precious little ones are taken away like that. His biographer does not allow us to enter into the inner sanctum of their tears, anger and deep numbness of spirit. But reading between the lines of this family tragedy I see the secret of an archbishop whose conviction of the love of God fired his zeal for evangelism, making him a great Bishop of London before his translation to Canterbury. In a letter to a man searching for faith from a position of deep agnosticism Archibald wrote:

> I cannot but believe that if at present you claim for yourself the name of atheist and materialist, a time will come when you will perceive and gladly acknowledge that Man is distinguished from brute creation by something higher than a

finer organisation of his material frame and that there is a
Being higher than Man who watches over him in life and in
death with a Father's love.

Only someone who has experienced such love even in the
context of personal tragedy can write like that.

The dialogue with God goes on today. In my travels
as head of the Anglican Communion I have seen
Christian groups all over the world in living dialogue
with God about his purposes for them, and how they
may best be furthered. In a recent trip to Mozambique,
one of the poorest countries in the world, I was thus
inspired by our small Anglican Church there, led by
Bishop Dinis Singulane, who has been bishop for
twenty-one years and is only fifty-one now. Under his
leadership this poor church has a social commitment
that is unrivalled in that country. From working among
street boys and girls, to the establishing of schools,
orphanages and enterprising projects such as getting
people to hand in their machine guns and weapons of
war in exchange for sewing machines and bicycles, that
church is endeavouring to work with God in his work
of 'making all things new'.

The God who makes demands

Another essential of the nature of God as Person is that of
goodness – 'righteousness', to use the Biblical term. And
this goes with the reality of personhood. We are conscious
of the truth that moral accountability and spiritual identity are uniquely at the heart of what it is to be a person;
this, even in the face of our century's moral relativism and
lack of absolutes.

I am reflecting a great deal on this at the moment

because just a short while ago I initiated a debate in the House of Lords on moral values. (I wonder if this curious and yet precious chamber has survived in any form to your day!) The debate was about 'Morals and our schools', but in reality I addressed the worrying national drift towards moral uncertainty in which no rights and wrongs exist outside the individual's personal tastes. The debate received widespread attention and support. It clearly struck a chord. The reason it did so is because deep down in each of us is an acceptance that a 'moral sense' is essential to our humanity. It is the tacit assumption of our laws that persons are capable of knowing the distinction between wrongdoing and keeping the law. Similarly, minors and those mentally unfit to plead are excused as not being capable of personal moral judgement. Christians have always seen this gift of moral and spiritual discrimination as an aspect of our personhood which most clearly reflects our divine likeness.

If then we may talk of this moral sense as a gift, a consequence of such a gift is that it must be used. God requires of us that we exercise our spiritual and moral faculties in both private and public life. That is why the demand that Christians should not speak in the name of their faith about the conduct of the nation's public affairs is so misconceived. God who is Person, and whose nature requires righteousness, demands of his human creation that they should exercise a moral discrimination rooted in his. That is what so much of the two-way dialogue between God and his people is about. Throughout both Old and New Testaments, through prophets and teachers and supremely in the Person of Christ, God speaks to us of our moral accountability to him and each other, and of our spiritual identity underlying this. The dialogue I have described earlier as running through the Church's history

– and it is just as sharp and urgent today – is fuelled by this reality: the dialogue between God and humanity on the calling to be 'good'. A great American writer of our century, Saul Bellow, a Nobel prize winner for literature, once created a character for whom this prayer was said at his death:

> Remember, God, the soul of Elya Grunner, who as willingly as possible and as well as he was able . . . was eager . . . to do what was required of him. . . . He was aware that he must meet, and he did meet – through all the confusion and degraded clowning of this life through which we are speeding – he did meet the terms of his contract. The terms which, in his inmost heart, each man knows. As I know mine. As all know. For that is the truth of it – that we all know, God, that we know, that we know, we know, we know.

In personal likeness to our Creator, we know what it is to make moral and spiritual choices with love as their basis. In personal likeness to our Creator, we live in relationship, expressed in dialogue and in shared choice and action. In personal likeness to him, we look for a fulfilling of that good purpose which underlies the creation of the cosmos itself. As we enter into that purpose, both as individuals and as the Church, something of the awesome depth of the goodness of the divine personhood becomes more open to us. Our love is mingled with wonder and marvelling. For here the 'personal' and the 'holy' meet.

And so we come to God as transcendent. And that is so great a subject that I must leave it to my next Letter. For I am due this day to go with Eileen on Retreat; that is to say, we are going to spend a week in prayer and reflection. We make a Retreat every year and without it my work – the work of both of us – would be barren and ineffective. It is ironic that so important an element in the Christian life is described by so misleading a term as a 'Retreat'. In my experience it is an 'advance'; an advance into the mystery of God who as Person delights in revealing his love, goodness and grace to all who come to him.

Your friend in God's purposes,

George

LETTER 4

The Holy God

Dear Friends of the Future,

I mentioned in my last Letter that Eileen and I were about to go on our annual Retreat; we have just returned refreshed and ready for the fray again. We usually go to a house maintained by a Contemplative Order of nuns. Their mother house is in Oxford, but they have a place of blessed silence and prayer called Bede House, which is down in Kent, and it is a truly wonderful resource to us both. It is a holy place, made so by the prayer and focus upon God of those devoted nuns who have given their lives to God. As I said before I often find the word 'Retreat' a misnomer because the last thing you do there is retreat! The kind of Retreat we were making is often hard work as you give yourself to prayer and spiritual scrutiny. Above all it is a time of renewal where you seek God and his strength for the battle ahead.

As I look at my Church today I am immensely impressed by the raw energy of much of church life which, in its own way, shows that the Church is in good

71

heart. Yet I do have a concern that this energy is not always anchored firmly into the deep roots of prayer and spiritual renewal which our great religious communities can offer. I do so hope that in your day there is a revival of this dimension of church life. And this leads me into the main theme of this Letter. I want to focus our attention on the notion of holiness, and in particular the holiness of God.

Most of us know of places that for one reason or another we feel to be holy. Sometimes it is because of the great deeds done for God in a place, lives given in martyrdom: my own Cathedral at Canterbury comes to mind, with not one but six martyred archbishops in its history. And places are sanctified – made holy – by lives of faith, as well as by the blood of believers shed there. One such place is very precious to me, and I learned to draw strength from it when I lived and worked in the North East. I used to resort to Lindisfarne, or Holy Island as it is better known, where Saint Aidan and Saint Cuthbert have left a tradition of holiness which is still alive in the area. Thousands of pilgrims, from every sort of church and none, come there regularly to seek strength.

When people come to such a place for its holiness, it is not, of course, Cuthbert or Aidan or Thomas Becket themselves they are seeking. It is the holy God who is being sought, and the holy lives and deaths of his followers are perceived as guides on the way, often felt to be more accessible by going to the places most associated with them. Hence, supremely, the millions of pilgrims to 'the Holy City', Jerusalem. The holy God is associated powerfully with such places, and so, it is claimed by many, he is to be experienced there in a direct and particular way which for many does not seem to happen elsewhere. So still, even in our current secularised society, pilgrims flow to the holy places, the great cathedrals, the islands of Lindisfarne, Iona, Whithorn . . .

Such journeyings are a response to our sense of, and hunger for, the holy: a seeking for something that answers to that awareness within ourselves of the numinous, the other-worldly. It is often urged by non-believers that 'God' is simply a projection of our imaginations. The truth is both simpler and deeper than that. What draws men and women to the holy places is an acknowledgement of other ways of 'knowing' beside those of material perception, or even of reasoning. Imagination is one means of knowing. What is important is the way it is used: there are right and wrong ways of 'imagining'. Honesty is the touchstone. Imagination becomes a false guide when we persuade ourselves, out of a personal longing, that something is so when it is not. On the other hand, imagination can lead us into sensitivities, to something beyond our previous awareness, when we are prepared to be honestly open; so that we are led, as Wordsworth once put it,

> to feelings that are not our own,
> And think, at random and imperfectly indeed,
> On man, the heart of man, and human life.

And it is this kind of knowing, through the quickened imagination, which opens us to a sensitivity to the holy; to what our instincts to worship and awe have as their proper focus. That is what we are tuning in to when we are drawn to the holy places of the world.

The holy God

And it is the holiness of God, quite as much as those aspects of him as Person I was talking about in my last Letter, which permeates such places and draws people to them. So I want to dwell on that in this Letter, not least because it is the extra and defining dimension of everything anyone can ever say or know about God. If we turn back to the Bible again, we'll find that from its beginning it never allows what it says of God as Person to overshadow its sense of his transcendence and holiness. It avoids on the one hand the over-stress on his immanence, which occurs when (as in some religions) God is not only identified with but subsumed in physical realities. On the other hand, it eschews the kind of Deism popular, for instance, in the eighteenth century, which by denying his personal, ongoing involvement in his Creation, suggests a complete transcendence untouched by compassion. The God of our faith as we meet him in the Bible is both *personal*, as close to us as the person we most love, and yet *wholly other*, Lord of all.

It is important that in our thinking about God we remain true to this Biblical balance. For, as I hinted at one point in my last Letter, the more powerfully we express our sense of God as Person, the greater risk we run of approximating too closely to human categories. Many people feel a strong and valid reaction against such an apparent 'domesticising' of God. (That is why patterns of worship which seem to address him over-familiarly are so unacceptable to some.) The Bible avoids this danger by making it plain that God is ultimately beyond human description: he is spiritual in his being, transcending human words and knowledge. As C. S. Lewis once prayed:

> Take not, Oh Lord, our literal sense. Lord, in Thy great
> Unbroken speech our limping metaphor translate.

It is such an indescribable Being, spiritually beyond our conceiving, of whom we have also spoken in terms of engagement with humanity in love and goodness. The

Old and New Testaments are consistent in this. When
Peter writes, 'As he who called you is holy, so be holy in
all you do; for it is written, "Be holy, because I am holy"'
(1 Peter 1:15–16) he is completely in accord, not only with
the book of Leviticus from which he is quoting, but with
the great eighth- and seventh-century writers such as
Hosea, Amos, Isaiah and Jeremiah, who were powerfully
to develop this sense of God as majestic in his spiritual
holiness, beyond human description: 'I am God, and not
man – the Holy One among you' (Hosea 11:9).

They were able to do this without destroying the
important link between God's transcendence and his
immanence by insisting, as Peter insisted, as indeed our
Lord insisted, that the love and righteousness which
bring him so closely into our lives as we respond to God
as Person, are inseparable from his holiness. Or, to put it
another way, his holiness is the source of his love and
'goodness'. When, for instance, Isaiah was seized with his
vision of God, 'high and lofty', it is above all God's holiness which overwhelms him. As the attendant seraphs
called to one another, 'Holy, holy, holy is the Lord of hosts;
the whole earth is full of his glory' it is his own impurity
– his moral and spiritual inadequacy – which appals the
prophet. And it is the burning coal from the holy fire on
the altar which symbolically is used in the vision to
prepare him to deliver to his people God's demands of
justice and love: 'This has touched your lips; your guilt is
taken away and your sin atoned for' (Isaiah 6:7). So, purified and charged with the aweful holiness of God, he is
charged also with what that means for the personal life of
God's people: justice and truth.

Amos was to give much the same message. Rejecting all
false holiness of ritual worship which bore no fruit in the
moral life of the nation, he spoke of God's demand

instead for sacrifices of holiness in life: 'But let justice roll on like a river, righteousness like a never-failing stream' (Amos 5:24). So the internalising of holiness by humanity has moral consequences rooted in the love learned from the holy love of God. Robert Herrick expressed it so beautifully:

> Is this a fast, to keep
> The larder lean?
>   And clean
> From fat of veals and sheep? . . .
>
> It is to fast from strife
> And old debate,
>   And hate;
> To circumcise thy life.
>
> To show a heart grief-rent;
>   To starve thy sin,
>   Not bin;
> And that's to keep thy Lent.

This is one of the most sharply defining characteristics of the Christian (as of the Jewish) God. The concept of holiness does not in all religions necessarily involve ethical implications. But from the first, in the history of our faith as God's people learned of him, his holiness was bound up with ethical questions; so that the characteristics which made it possible to speak of God as Person not only were not in conflict with speaking of his holiness, but actually rooted in it.

'Thou only art holy'

We need to keep this at the back of our minds as we return to considering more fully God's transcendence. How does the Bible convey to us One who is ultimately beyond human description? How does it convey his 'beyond-ness', if I can put it like that? Of its many different methods I want to pick out just three for you to think about, not least because I think they still address our times, and almost certainly will have something to say to yours.

(i) Distance

First, nowhere, even in the Old Testament, is there any trace of the suggested equality between God and human beings that one finds, for instance, in the myths of Greece, Babylonia, Egypt and Rome, where the deity is pictured in terms realistically human in style (and not always of the noblest quality). By contrast, even at his most intimate when engaged with the people he has chosen and loves, the God of the Old Testament is wholly 'other'. Take, for example, Moses' encounter with the God who is to be revealed to him as 'Yahweh' (Exodus 3:14). In it, God speaks with Moses in the most intimate human terms, encouraging, scolding, rebuking, even bargaining. Yet all this happens in the context of the revelation of the holy name, 'Yahweh', *One Who Will Be*, by the mysterious burning bush (compare the other glimpses we get of the holy fire which burns but does not consume, such as the faithful in the 'burning fiery furnace' [Daniel 3:24–28] or, supremely, the tongues of flame at Pentecost [Acts 2:1–4]). And Moses' sense of being addressed directly by God in a situation of awe-inspiring holiness is unequivocal: 'Do not come any closer . . . Take off your sandals, for the place where you are standing is holy ground.' And this reminds us that even in our most intimate moments with God there is not, and never can be, equity. And to try to claim it falsifies the relationship.

(ii) Revelation of new names for God

The awe attaching to this first revelation of one of the holy names of God underlies the second way in which the Bible's account of God maintains his 'otherness'. That is, the experiences that his people have of encounter with him are so profound that they point beyond ordinary experience to a deeper reality, a meeting with a being at some more searching level. This continues to be the case right through to today, and, I dare guess, goes on being true for your generation also. In the early days of the United Nations, Dag Hammerskjöld, one of its early and greatest General Secretaries, noted the same experience in his private diary, published after his death:

> I don't know Who – or what – put the question, I don't know when it was put. I don't even remember answering. But at some moment I did answer Yes to Someone – or Something – and from that hour I was certain that existence is meaningful and that, therefore, my life, in self-surrender, had a goal.

One of the ways the Bible gives content to such encounters with the holy God is, as we have seen in the call of Moses, by revealing in them new aspects of God's nature by disclosing new holy names by which he might be truly known. Revealing a name is a potent symbol in these early Old Testament cultures, since one's very being, the whole integrity of one's character, is focused in it. So, for instance, in God's dealings with Abraham. As Abraham goes out in faith from his homeland to follow the mysterious God who leads him onwards, so God reveals more to him of his divine nature by disclosing new names: 'El Elyon' – God Most High (Genesis 14:19); 'El Roi' – God Who Sees (Genesis 16:13); 'El Shaddai' – God Almighty (Genesis 17:1); 'Jehovah Jireh' – the Provider (Genesis 22:14).

It is worth pondering what new names for himself God has revealed to us. The latter half of this century, for instance, has opened up to us the need to recognise that holy names for God which imply maleness are to be complemented by names which reveal, in his divine wholeness, an equivalent femaleness. So we are with confidence able to talk of God as Father and Mother. This is, of course, not to imply that gender is in any sense an attribute of God. Language about God, as we noted earlier, is essentially analogical. God is God: beyond human categories of gender or anything else. But the discovery of the holy name of God as Mother arises from insights given us which have hitherto been either ignored or, though known, under-emphasised. Starting from a profounder recognition of what it means that the whole of humanity is 'made in the image of God', female and male alike, we are led to ponder what this discloses to us of the nature of God. It is then that we are prepared to look afresh into the way Biblical language is used, and thus discover depths and riches which point to the whole breadth of human life, female as well as male, imaging the glory of the holy God in his love and goodness. We find it in the Old Testament, particularly in certain passages from Isaiah. Most clearly of all we find it in the New Testament, in, for instance, the way Jesus himself is reported as overturning traditional God-language. He speaks of God as 'Abba' – the tenderest possible title for 'Father'; he replaces patriarchal, hierarchical models with those of service and love, the relationships most associated with women; and women are so significant among his disciples that they are listed by name as at the foot of the Cross and as the first discerners of the Resurrection wonder.

Moreover, Jesus directly used stories about women in

his teaching. There are in Luke 15 three parallel stories told by Jesus to show something of God's nature: of the lost sheep and the caring shepherd, the lost coin and the caring woman, the lost son and the caring father. How revealing that until latterly we have heard so little exposition of the story concerning the woman and the coin! Similarly, while we have dwelt at length on the picture in the Gospel of John of the Father sending the Logos, the Word, into the world (John 1:18), it is only in these latter days that we have begun to ponder the theological implications of the language, in that same Gospel, of 'giving birth'. So, slowly, a new holy name of God has been given to us; analogical, like all the other ones revealed. What new name has he revealed to *you*? Don't be surprised if in your day you are learning new things about the God we worship.

(iii) The holy God must not be blasphemed in worship or by lifestyle

A third way in which the Bible conveys God's 'beyondness', certainly in the Old Testament, is in its sharp prohibition against the making of religious images. It is one of the fundamental rules of faithfulness to God, spelled out in the Ten Commandments: 'You shall not make for yourself an idol in the form of anything in heaven above or on the earth beneath' (Exodus 20:4). Behind this lies something true for every century – including your own, whatever the changes and insights which are now yours. For such a commandment was requiring of the faithful a recognition that the glory of God could be falsified and domesticated, which meant risking the sin of blasphemy.

We need to pause here to reflect on this a little further. The Commandments by such a prohibition were saying something both about the holiness of God, and the frailty of humanity in relation to that holiness. Of God they were indicating that the glory of his holiness is so absolute that any attempt at delineation becomes, inevitably, a parody. That is why holiness is always at the risk of blasphemy; since blasphemy is an act of irreverence towards the holy. (Which is why in any healthy society the law of the land takes blasphemy seriously.) And of humanity the Commandments were saying that human religious practice carries always within it the seeds of its own corruption, even in the most 'spiritual' of faiths, because there is always the temptation to fall into the snare of formalism, of an externalised religion. (See, for instance, the regression to the worship of the golden calf, in Moses' absence [Exodus 32].) That is why the most holy God must never be thought of as wholly localised, in thing or in place or ritual or in person. Hence the vehement rejection of any object that could be seen as an idol in the Old Testament; hence Christ's own insistence that even the sacred places such as the Temple at Jerusalem must never be seen as defining the area of God's accessible holiness; and hence, of course, the horror of the pious Jews at Christ's own divine claims. The glory of the holiness of God, both Old and New Testaments insist, is best discerned in his presence in the heart. So Moses, though he longs to see the full glory of God (Exodus 33:18) may not do so, but can only perceive it *after it has passed:* but God comforts him that he will know of that glory within himself: 'My presence will go with you, and I will give you rest.' What we need to remember, in understanding the content of that promise, is that God's presence with his people, and in particular with Moses, had been marked by the presence of the 'shekinah cloud', the cloud of the glory of God's holiness, resting on the tent of meeting:

As Moses went into the tent, the pillar of cloud would come down and stay at the entrance, while the Lord spoke with Moses. Whenever the people saw the pillar of cloud standing at the entrance to the tent, they all stood and worshipped, each at the entrance to his tent. The Lord would speak to Moses face to face, as a man speaks with his friend. (Exodus 33:9–11a)

So God's promise of his presence is a promise of the personal experience of the glory of his holiness. Precisely the same is implied by Christ's own words about the holiest place to worship:

Believe me . . . a time is coming when you will worship the Father neither on this mountain nor in Jerusalem . . . a time is coming and has now come when the true worshippers will worship the Father in spirit and truth, for they are the kind of worshippers the Father seeks. God is spirit, and his worshippers must worship in spirit and in truth. (John 4:21, 23)

Such understandings are gathered up in the account of Christ's Transfiguration 'on the holy mountain', when the glory of God's holiness brings together what has been revealed through Moses, through the prophets, and through Christ, so that briefly the chosen disciples glimpse it. It is too much for them: they are overcome by the glory, and they do not know how to respond. But the reality of that glory of holiness is unquestionable, and becomes in due course part of their understanding.

I have to say, sadly, that our history as a Church has shown a tendency to swing between over-emphasising either God's remoteness or his nearness. And in this century I think the continued flow of people to holy places, and the many who seek what some of the Eastern religions offer of mysteriousness and awe, all point to a strong reaction against our Western loss of a sense of reverence, a willingness to feel awe. The inability of so many to see that the word 'blasphemy' could have content in the twentieth century, or that people may be right in being profoundly disturbed at the deepest level by books or films which portray central matters or figures of faith sacriligiously – such blunting of the capacity for sensitivity to holiness is a sign of a much diminished and narrowed culture. Perhaps by your time, my dear friends of the future, we shall as a society have recovered that essential instinct for holiness, so that the pilgrims of holiness are not over against the drift of their times, but enacting moments of reverence on behalf of a society which values them. I hope so, and I pray so; for I do believe a nation's health depends on it.

Yahweh – the Covenant God

The revelation Moses received in the desert by the burning bush, of the holy name of God, was a foretaste and promise of what this God was to be to Moses' people. 'Yahweh' is a virtually untranslatable word. It is best approached, while acknowledging that it is mysterious and is meant to be, by recognising that it is rooted in the Hebrew verb 'to be', especially its future tense: 'I will be what I will be'. What God was to be to his people – and still is and ever will be – is given substance in the deliverance from Egypt and the making of a holy nation. In the history and faith of Israel the revelation of the name was the inner reality of the dramatic event of victory over Egypt, which is for ever commemorated in the annual feast of the Passover. As Israel prepared to escape Egypt, God's direction was that the people should sprinkle sacrificial lamb's blood on their door lintels (Exodus 12:7) and this would be their protection as Yahweh passed over the land in judgement. The meaning of the story is clear: God's people are thus 'blood-purchased', secured by the blood of sacrifice. It is a foretaste of that greater deliverance with which he has delivered 'a multitude, whom no man can number'. In the giving of his name, God revealed himself as a Covenant God who would be Redeemer of a people in faith relationship with him.

That Covenant was ratified on Mount Sinai. With it, God's people were led into a new lifestyle of holy living and of a worship true to the one God who had made himself known to them. The nature of God as he had disclosed it in his mighty acts and in his guidance of his people, was one of 'loving-kindness' – *hesed* – the practical outpouring of love for his people. And that love was, as the rich Biblical vocabulary expressing it suggests, a sacrificial love, the language of sacrifice suggesting the giving of oneself for the other; or the 'cleaving to someone' above all else. But his nature was also one of righteousness, that pure goodness I spoke of in my last Letter. It means a relationship of mutually right conduct. It means a relationship of mutually right worship. It means, in fact, a covenanted relationship of divine self-giving and human response.

We are back to that human 'contract' again which I spoke of at the end of my last Letter to you: of 'the terms of his contract', which at heart every person knows, 'For that is the truth of it . . . that we know, we know, we know.'

And hence the question arises: What happens if – when – we break the contract: are we to abandon the Covenant? Does a righteous God abandon it also? Or are there deeper depths of justice and love in the holiness of this God of ours, such that he can find a way to resolve the hopeless confronting of the integrity of justice with the compassion of love? That is the astonishing Christian experience of the holiness of God. And the only way to enter that is to meet Jesus. I spoke at the beginning of this Letter about the unknowability of the holy God. But in his Son, the Lord Jesus Christ, we are promised we may come near, and meet him. So that is what I want to tell you about in my next Letter. Before then I shall have celebrated Easter in my own Cathedral at Canterbury, and been seized again with what the holiness of God actually means, of justice and mercy, of righteousness and love, for the human race. So – though you may be reading this at some quite other season – I wish you, across the generations, all joy and hope in the holy God at Easter time.

Your friend in that holy Covenant,

LETTER 5

Finding Out About Jesus

Dear Friends of the Future,

My regular route to the M1 takes me past the beautiful building on the edge of Regent's Park which clearly images the kind of multi-layered society we now are. The Regent's Park Mosque declares eloquently two things. First, that religious faith today in Britain – faith in the one God – is not to be measured simply in terms of membership of the Christian denominations. There is a commonality of religious experience between the adherents of church, synagogue and mosque which must be taken most seriously and cherished as something which can, and should, be bonding. Yet it also states that there are between us essential differences of religious understanding, and the experience of God which gives rise to that understanding – differences which must not be papered over or swept aside in our inter-faith coming together.

I dream that by your day, my dear fellow Christians of the future, great advances will have been made in the inter-faith ecumenical journey, as in all other ecumenical experience. Meanwhile, the Regent's Park Mosque reminds me of the God we share but also of the God we do not. Where is this difference essentially located? It is in our experience and knowledge of Jesus Christ. So it is of him, and why our experience of God is so radically different because of him, that I want to write to you now.

The importance of Jesus

Why is it that Jesus is so vital to our faith as Christians? Why do we long that all should encounter him? Why is it that beyond anything else I pray that you who are to come should know him and be secured by him?

At one level the answer is obvious, for in the Christian world Jesus is the centre of human history; indeed we separate history between those events that happened 'BC' (before Christ) and those that occurred after his birth 'AD' (Anno Domini – In the Year of Our Lord). As I write this we are approaching the Millennium. It has been important to remind people that all the proposed Millennium celebrations and activities draw their significance, in the end, from the impact of Jesus Christ on our world in the first century and celebrated ever since by the Church that bears his name.

However, as enormously important as that matter of dating is (and more so than many people have given thought to), it is but the external sign of something much profounder, at the heart of our Christian understanding of 'Life, the Universe and Everything' (to quote part of the title of a very popular book in the bookstores as I write). Christ is the heart and the life-blood of our Christian faith and therefore the very source of that by which we live. As the writer of the First Epistle of John put it sharply: 'Who is the liar? It is the man who denies that Jesus is the Christ.

Such a man is the antichrist – he denies the Father and the Son' (2:22). That verse expresses with passion what to many in my day – secularists, for instance, or adherents of other faiths – seems the unacceptable face of Christianity. It is called the 'scandal of particularity'; that is to say, the conviction that in Jesus God has appeared finally and fully. Or, as David Jenkins, one of our best-known and most controversial bishops, put it simply and powerfully recently: that Christians believe that, 'In the Incarnation God spoke his last and final word about absolutely everything . . . and that word is one of hope.'

So finding out about God's 'last word about absolutely everything' is clearly of first importance. For we are speaking of the God I wrote of in my earlier Letters, the God on whom the life of the whole cosmos, and all within it, depends. How are we to know more of his 'last word'? In the end, of course, it is by personal encounter with this Jesus. He is to be known today, alive and active in our lives, as he will be in yours, not simply as a 'remembered figure' but as a Person to know as intimately as we know those we love best.

But how are we to achieve such knowledge? How are we to meet him? Where is he to be known?

Faith and history

There are three main ways through which human beings meet Jesus, although one has to admit that there is no limit to the variety of ways in which he discloses himself. The three main ways are these: he reveals himself personally to individuals (as he did to me so many years ago when I started out on the Christian journey); he reveals himself through being with his people when they are worshipping him; and he reveals himself through the study of the primary accounts of him which we call the New Testament. I shall leave to one side the first two ways of meeting and knowing Jesus because we shall consider aspects of these ways later. At this point I want to concentrate on what is involved in finding out about him through the records of his life and work through the primary source, the New Testament.

As I do so it is important to remember that we are talking about the one whom millions of people have known or know personally, for we cannot properly make sense of the history, the life story, of Jesus without taking account of the faith life of his followers – both his first followers, such as those who wrote the Gospels, and those who follow him today. As Dr Eric Mascall, a great Anglican theologian, wrote some years ago:

> What we need to know and can know about Jesus is what we in fact already know about him as members of his Church . . . It is paradoxically important to know what Jesus said and did in his earthly life because it is substantially what he is experienced as being and doing today . . . For some, arising from the reading or the preaching of scripture . . . For others, through sacramental shared life. In both cases the experience, whilst it is emphatically not an event in the distant past, is undetachable from certain events described in the Gospels.

In that famous statement Dr Mascall argues for continuity. The Lord we know today is the same Jesus who lived in Palestine long ago. Mascall's central argument is that experience today must relate to historical evidence concerning Jesus. How can we be sure?

Approaches to the New Testament

The New Testament, our primary source for approaching the question of knowing Jesus, is itself a complex of material. Over the years there has been much dispute about how to read it. From the mid-eighteenth century to my day there have been scholars who have argued that the main gospel accounts of Jesus must be treated sceptically. Indeed, *The Quest for the Historical Jesus* (the title of a brilliant book by Albert Schweitzer) can be said in one sense to have begun with the approach that, in reality, there is little we can know about the Jesus of history. Another scholarly view was that Jesus was simply a political/religious revolutionary who died a failure, but his followers stole his body and later wrote stories about his being the great redeemer expected by the nation; and a later figure, Paul, refashioned the whole thing into a religious belief system. If that sounds familiar to you it is because the same dramatic so-called 'discoveries' are peddled as 'new' and 'faith shattering' at fairly regular intervals. In my time as Archbishop we've had quite a season of such 'revelations' on TV as well in bookshops and in scholarly seminars. These 'revelations' vary in quality of scholarship – some use quite seriously rigorous scholarship, while others owe more to imagination than truth. While both are ultimately seeking to take the mystery out of Christ, in fact they bear indirect witness to it, in showing that we cannot avoid the impact of that extraordinary personality whose huge shadow still falls across our century.

However, there are two attitudes in any discussion of how to read the New Testament in order to find out about Jesus which I want to urge as by their very nature false. They should be spurned by your generation as by mine. The first is the attitude I have just started discussing in which total scepticism is the starting point; an attitude which begins from a conviction that the Gospels *cannot be* in any sense factually true. The second is equally spurious: that the New Testament lies above historical research, that because it is God-inspired it is improper to use our intellects to dig deep into the structure and development of books we love and know so well.

Neither approach is fruitful. Total scepticism, for instance, denies by its very nature the neutrality it claims. No writer, in fact, is ever neutral. It is not a position possible to hold, since all writers are sifting evidence from a particular point of view. That's a truth which historians now accept. And of course total scepticism has to find some way of accommodating the extraordinary impact of Jesus, not only during his own time, but through twenty centuries since. Furthermore, the argument which was often the basis of scepticism in approaching the Gospels (that they were written long after the events they describe and were therefore the 'myth-creation' of the early Church) is now largely exploded. For the patient work of scholars has made it clear that it is not the case that the New Testament was written long after the events described. A substantial section of the first three Gospels, for example, reflects 'handed-down' stories, parables and narratives about Jesus that must have found their expression almost contemporaneously. This material forms the bulk of what we know as the Synoptic Gospels (i.e. those three Gospels – Matthew, Mark and Luke – which when 'seen together' reveal similar stories and structure). The Synoptic Gospels are supplemented by the Gospel of John, generally regarded as being written later, and by many of the epistles which were written before the Gospels (between AD 47 and 62). The argument based on inaccuracy because of time gap, therefore, won't safely hold.

But equally, the total rejection of historical research based on the assumption that sacred texts must not be subjected to historical criticism won't hold either. For instance, the fact that we have four Gospels illustrates the problem; four accounts 'about all that Jesus began to do and to teach until the day he was taken up to heaven', as Luke describes the intention and scope of his Gospel (Acts 1:1–2). Even though the three Synoptics' writers are dealing with what is obviously the same tradition and material, there are quite important differences in the way they present it. And when you compare what *they* have to say with John's account, there are major differences that demand exploration and study. Why, for example, does John group the miracles in seven great 'signs' which reveal Jesus to be the Messiah? Why does he omit so many of the Synoptic stories of Jesus which we can presume he knew? Why is the Last Supper recorded in John quite significantly differently from the version of the other three writers, with no command to eat bread and drink wine 'in memory of me'? This strange fact is made more mysterious by the fact that there are passages in his Gospel which are obviously 'sacramental'. These differences – and there are so many – simply cannot be ignored.

I have laboured this point to show how vital it is to study with all scholarly tools available the differences as well as the identities in the accounts of Jesus. For we lose the marvellous richness of our New Testament inheritance if we fear to explore its complexity. What we are dealing with is neither plain history (there is no such thing) nor faith statements (myths, as some have called them) unrelated to fact. Nor are we dealing with simple biography either (although it does not surprise us to learn that in style and structure the gospel story is very like a number of first-century biographies on famous people). Rather we are handling a type of literature that we could call 'theological biography'.

Tools used in discovering who Jesus is

Over the last two centuries two major tools, form criticism and redaction criticism, have been developed for handling this rich complexity of New Testament material. *Form criticism* is the study of the putative 'pre-history' of the New Testament. It asks questions like: How did the stories and individual units of the Gospels come to be collected and written? How within each document were its different elements fused together? *Redaction criticism* concerns itself with identifying the distinctive theology of each document, bearing in mind what I said earlier, that there is no such thing as plain history. So redaction criticism asks: How has the theology of the individual writer shaped the selection of the material and even the setting of the stories?

These Letters are clearly not the place to go into the details of these tools, but as they lie behind some of the things I want to describe to you, it has been necessary to glance at the way scholarship has developed.

Let us now go back to Albert Schweitzer, whose aim to discover the historical Jesus was so formative for later thought. Schweitzer – missionary, musician and theologian – was a man of deep faith, keen to ask: How much can we really know about the Jesus of history? His conclusion was that although we can know much about the 'Jesus of faith', nothing of the historical Jesus was recoverable. The closing words of his impressive book remain searching to my own day, possibly even to yours: 'He comes to us as One unknown without a name, as of old, by the lakeside he came to those men who knew him not. He speaks to us the same word "Follow thou me" and sets us to the tasks which he has to fulfil for our time . . . and, as in an ineffable mystery, they shall learn in their experience who he is.'

However, what was a serious lack in post-Schweitzer studies was a disconnecting of the actions of Jesus (what he did) from the teaching of Jesus (what he said). The assumption of so many scholars was that the work of unknown followers of Jesus has made it impossible to penetrate beyond their interpretations to discover for ourselves the true Christ. Yet this has not deterred many of them from speculations which seem tenuous and even tendentious. For instance, four distinct interpretations have emerged: (i) Jesus the Failed Revolutionary – both religious and political, confronting either Rome or the Temple system; (ii) Jesus the Supreme Ethical Teacher, who through his teachings has given the world the shape of a morality based on love; (iii) Jesus the Leader, who was calling people of all races and nations to a new fellowship; and (iv) Jesus the Apocalyptic Herald, foretelling in accordance with Jewish expectation the imminent end of the world.

Needless to say, each of these theories contains aspects of truth. But none contains the entire truth and, every decade or so, these interpretations of Christ come back with almost predictable regularity, dressed up in new terminology suggesting they are entirely new ideas.

Yet, it is important to recognise that we owe much to those scholars whose scholarship has helped us to understand the complexities of the New Testament material. For instance, it was through one of these scholars, Holtzmann, that the question 'What kind of documents were the Gospels?' was firmly linked with 'What can we know about Jesus?'. Incidentally, it was he who first argued that Mark's was the earliest Gospel, now something generally agreed, which has profound consequences for our understanding of the three Synoptic Gospels. Another scholar, Johannes Weiss, insisted on studying Jesus in the context of his own day. He pointed out that the kingdom of God at the time of Jesus would not have been understood as referring to 'good and kindly living' but to the imminent action of God in history and the end of the world. I shall be writing to you about the Last Things in (of course!) my last Letter.

The other issue, by far the most crucial, was how far faith and history need to relate at all. Here the idea was developed that there was no necessary categorical relation between the 'experience' of faith and the 'realities' of history. This thread of religion detached from historical fact has run through our culture, both literary and theological, ever since the mid-nineteenth century.

But the logical consequence of this was obvious. Once faith had been disconnected from history it was inevitable that there would be later scholars who would argue that there was no need to search for the historic Jesus anyway. Bultmann, for example, believed the existential call to 'decision' to be sufficient. That was the hallmark of the 'faith-cult' that had grown from the 'Jesus story'. The Word event did not have to be connected to historical events. The search to find the authentic sayings of Jesus through form criticism and redaction criticism was for Bultmann and others a failed and unnecessary enterprise. I am myself quite clear that the question which remains the crucial issue for Christians of my day and possibly for yours is: *Is our faith rooted in history or are the Gospels simply pious fictions?* It does not seem to me possible to overstate the importance of the relationship between the actual historic event of the man Jesus – what he said, did and achieved – and the faith we share with each other, with the Church of the past and with you who are to come.

And indeed, as I write, there has been a swing again to this view, with some writers insisting that when the

Church worships its Lord that act must relate to the historical Person Jesus who lived in first-century Palestine. Work still continues on trying to determine the authenticity of the sayings of Jesus (there is now a 'Jesus Seminar' in the States where American scholars meet to seek agreement by voting on questions of historicity and so on). In the meantime a number of contemporary scholars have laid the basis for a sound and scholarly hermeneutic (principles for interpreting the New Testament) which should point the way forward for scholars of your day.

Some key questions about the Jesus of history

One of our current leading scholars, N. T. Wright, has recently summed up for us what the key questions now appear to be as we think about the Jesus of his day.

First, what aspirations of contemporary Judaism did Jesus share and what did he challenge? Did he stand over against everything in it and, if not, what did he challenge, and why?

Second, what were Jesus' own aims? In terms of day-to-day ministry, what set his priorities and took him from A to B? Linked to this, what did Jesus want people to do to respond to him appropriately (that is to say, not only following his death but in his own time with them in Palestine)?

Third, Dr Wright asks about the death of Jesus. What reasons justified such a violent death? On the one hand there are those who insist, against the evidence, that Jesus was a political revolutionary and it was therefore inevitable that the Romans would have to kill him. On the other hand, there are those who present Jesus in such bland terms as a kind of mild, holy man, that it becomes incredible that anyone would want to crucify someone so

inoffensive. The truth has to lie somewhere in between –
but where?

Finally, why did the early Church begin? (In other
words, what happened between Jesus' burial in the tomb
and the bursting out of the young Church on the streets at
Pentecost?) That is to say: What really happened that first
Easter? What is indisputable is that Jesus actually died
and that quite against the grain a powerful new faith
emerged from that death. What was it?

We cannot avoid approaching these events as history as
well as faith experiences because they are a vital part of
Jesus' own personal history. This then takes us back to our
starting point: we can only begin to tackle these questions
properly if we recognise the Gospels as biographies
written from a theological perspective – histories written
with the understanding of faith, but still *histories*. And
because there are four of them we shall get history with
four different selective principles operating; all sharing
the same faith in the Jesus they know but with different
theological and cultural ideas important to them.

And this is no new problem. We sometimes seem to
give the impression that it is only to the sophisticated
twentieth century that intelligent questions arise about
what truth lies behind or in the Gospels. Perhaps you in
the twenty-first century will be both humbler and, therefore, wiser. For as Professor Eric Mascall pointed out ten
years ago in his book *Jesus: Who He Is – and How We Know
Him*, which has proved to be a forerunner of the present
wave of 'Jesus' studies:

> the correct question is not how to bridge the gulf between the
> experience of the twentieth century Christian and the life of
> the first century Palestine Jew, Jesus (as if the 20th century
> was of unique importance). It is how to bridge the gulf
> between the experience of *any* Christian who did not see and

hear Jesus in the flesh and Jesus himself. The gulf has been bridged by the Church . . . fanning out from that unique event in space and time . . . the New Testament documents have a unique character and status as being the primary written product of the impact on mankind made by the eternal word becoming man. The basic hermeneutic problem – the problem of understanding and interpreting the incarnate word – arose when the accounts were first written, not now when we try to discover 'what lies behind the Gospels'.

And so, as I close this Letter, we have come to the point where we are ready to look at how the four Gospels differently illuminate some of the questions I have just summarised, as well as some of the basic ones listed earlier. In spite of all the sceptical questions I have sought to address in this Letter, there remains today a compulsive interest in the Person Jesus who continues to fascinate, intrigue and draw people with his teaching and wonderful life. Meanwhile, it is my pleasant task next week to leave my office and go to talk with some 20,000 or so young people gathered for the Greenbelt Festival who want to 'know more about Jesus'. And that is what I shall be writing about to you next.

Your brother in the name of the same Jesus of Nazareth,

LETTER 6

The Jesus of His Contemporaries

Dear Friends of the Future,

What an astonishing time I had at Greenbelt! Although a very cold and wet weekend, nothing could dampen the spirits of 20,000 young people who were there to celebrate their faith. I celebrated the Holy Communion service and also preached. I was most amused when following the service a young girl congratulated me on producing such an imaginative liturgy for Greenbelt. 'The words were so good,' she remarked. 'Just right for the style of Greenbelt.'

'Good,' I replied. 'But I am sorry to disappoint you. All I used was one of our normal services. It is from *The Alternative Service Book 1980!*'

Following lunch I was quizzed by 2,000 young people who asked me searching questions on practically every possible subject.

Since writing my last Letter I was uncomfortable that you might be thinking that all I was doing in it was raising difficult questions. Archbishops, after all, are here to give answers – aren't they? But I hope that the Letter helped

101

you to understand why often when Christians are asked what seems a perfectly straightforward question, like 'Did Jesus say he was God?', we have to clear the ground a bit as to what the question means and what kind of evidence we have.

In this Letter I want to stay with the questions about Jesus' life and ministry, focusing on how his contemporaries must have experienced this unusual Person. In the next Letter I shall address the matter of the first Easter and what happened then.

To begin at the beginning

'Begin at the beginning' and right away some of the difficulties I was outlining in my last Letter become obvious. We could begin with the Gospel of Mark, the first to be written down, which probably first appeared in Rome in the early 60s AD. Actually, although Mark was the first complete Gospel to tell the story of Jesus, we are in no doubt that fragments of sayings, stories and possibly parables were circulating earlier. Scholars refer to one set of stories as 'Q', a suppositional collection which formed the basis of the Synoptic Gospels. No doubt by the early 60s there was an urgent need for the complete story of Jesus to be made available. Mark provides it.

So Mark's Gospel is where we shall start. And where does he begin? Well, very much from the twin bases I was talking about, of both *faith* and *history*. His opening words are a faith statement: 'The beginning of the good news of Jesus Christ, the Son of God.' This sets out clearly the presupposition of all that follows: it is written from the perspective of faith by someone convinced of the truth of that faith; and that it is 'good news'.

And then we are plunged into history, into the impact

that two remarkable men made at a specific time and place on those around them. The first was to become known as 'John the baptiser' because what he taught and believed was focused in his action of calling people to the waters of repentance following their acknowledgement of sin. The other was to become known, eventually, as Jesus 'the Christ' – the holy one, the 'Messiah'. Mark introduces him as appearing suddenly on the scene as a remarkable man: he is baptised by John and then, after a desert experience, his ministry begins. No birth or childhood background, no genealogies. For Mark, the history of Jesus begins from his baptism and ministry. So Mark answers the question 'Who was Jesus?' very much in the way we do when we are asked about somebody. He tells us where he comes from – from Nazareth; and what he 'does' – he is a wandering preacher and teacher, a holy man. That's the 'beginning' as far as Mark is concerned.

Now, when we turn to Matthew and Luke, we find that they see the 'beginning' differently. Both give genealogies. In fact Matthew opens his whole account with one. And both give detailed birth stories, which are at the same time similar and dissimilar. It is clear that both Matthew and Luke want to show Jesus' formal connectedness with the human race through genealogy and through the actual birth process. At the same time they wish to show that Jesus also comes directly from God, hence the emphasis upon the virginal conception.

While Matthew and Luke have much in common we need to recognise the important theological differences. For example, Luke is clearly writing from a *non-Jewish* perspective. He does not start his Gospel with a genealogy but puts it at the same point from which Mark begins his whole account, at the point when Jesus is thirty years of age and about to commence his ministry. Luke precedes it with the birth stories and with an indication of what he is trying to do in his writing – that is, to set out an 'orderly account' of the events 'that have been fulfilled among us' so that his reader 'may know the certainty' (Luke 1:3–4). Luke locates the birth narratives at a specific time when the Roman Emperor had demanded that all conquered people returned to their homes for a census. So Luke sets his Gospel in world history. When he comes to his genealogy of Jesus he wishes to show that Jesus belongs to the whole human race, the son of seventy-six generations beginning with 'Adam, the son of God'. This is the Jesus whose impact on his immediate world is not confined to his own people but extends to all, including the despised Samaritans and the hated Romans.

The 'Jewishness' of Jesus

Matthew's genealogy, by contrast, is aimed at showing the impeccability of Jesus' *Jewish* pedigree. Matthew, like Mark, opens with a faith statement calling Jesus 'the Messiah', but for him the crucial beginning of the Jesus story is that he is 'the son of David, the son of Abraham'. His genealogy is a carefully stylised one to show it: fourteen generations from Abraham to David; fourteen generations from David to the deportation of the people of Israel to Babylon; and a final fourteen generations from the return from exile to the coming of the Messiah.

Now this is very important for us in grasping the impact of Jesus on his contemporaries. For it pushes directly into our consciousness something we tend to ignore – the Jewishness of Jesus. I don't mean by that merely his ethnic identity, but all that Jewishness meant in terms of first-century Palestine. If, thanks to the differing emphases of the New Testament writers, we are to catch a rounded, three-dimensional glimpse of Jesus, we ignore at our peril that for his followers and friends, Jesus was identified from the outset with his nation's hope. And what was that? One clue is in that reference to deportation to Babylon in the genealogy of Matthew. The scars of that were reopened by the Roman occupation under which Jesus was born. Although the Jewish people are no longer in exile, they are still bound and unfree in their own land. So naturally the long tradition of waiting and longing for the coming of the Deliverer of Israel was alive and running at the very time of Jesus' ministry.

This waiting took many different forms, as all waiting does. Some prepared for the coming of the Deliverer by political plotting; some by ever-greater zeal in keeping the Law, observing all the religious rules; others by looking for signs and wonders that might suggest the 'End' was nigh. Ordinary pious people suffered, waited and longed for release from the yoke of Rome. Most of us in our societies have never known enslavement of that kind (and I pray that the freedom we at present enjoy will continue to be a reality in your day too). But in my travels visiting Christians across the world, I have encountered people experiencing longing of that kind. I recall, for example, my visit to one of the refugee camps outside Khartoum and meeting hundreds of young mothers with their tiny offspring uprooted from their homes in the south and separated from husbands and the extended family. Their longing for home was reflected in their eyes and resounded in their songs.

But there's much more to Jesus' Jewishness than that. The point we must not forget is that of the Jewish nation's own self-perception in the time of Jesus – a perception which has remained constant, in spite of apostasy and exile – since Moses under God called the Israelites to become a nation under God's special guidance. This self-perception was to be a people appointed by God to be a channel of special blessing to the world. That was Israel's best hope, often distorted by spiritual arrogance on the one hand and backsliding on the other. Their destiny was to be instrumental to God's plans for all the nations. And the Jewishness of Jesus focused on this. If he was in some way to deliver his people, it must be in order that God's purposes through an obedient people should be fulfilled for the world.

'Are you the one who was to come?'

It is clear from the four Gospels that expectation in this profounder sense attached itself to Jesus from the beginning. In the birth stories in Matthew, Joseph is assured that this child 'will save his people from their sins' and will be an 'Emmanuel', 'God with us' to his people. He is connected with the prophecy of the 'king of the Jews' being born in Bethlehem. Luke's birth stories include not only the shepherds making known their mysterious experience but the prophecy of Simeon at his circumcision and of Anna, who 'gave thanks to God and spoke about the child to all who were looking forward to the redemption of Jerusalem' (Luke 2:38).

As Jesus' active ministry develops we catch glimpses of this expectation attached to Jesus through the response of others. John the Baptist, for example, in the Gospel of John, speaks of Jesus as 'the Lamb of God who takes away the sin of the world'. All the Gospels, in fact, record John's recognition of Jesus in terms of the expected deliverer. And there is a poignant moment in that expectation later, when from prison John sends a message to ask Jesus: 'Are you the one who was to come, or should we expect someone else?' (Luke 7:18).

So, the beginning, as described by the three accounts of

the Synoptic Gospels, opens for us at once both the world within which Jesus was moving and how that world perceived his role to be. But if we go for our beginning of the story to the Gospel of John we are in a different world. For John is not interested to the same degree with Jewish expectation but, rather, how this fits in with the world he wishes to address – namely the Greek/Gentile world of the Roman Empire. John therefore begins with the most comprehensive fusion of faith-statement and history, placing Jesus in a daring and awesome context of ownership of space and time: 'In the beginning was the Word, and the Word was with God, and the Word was God. Through him all things were made; without him nothing was made.'

And yet John never lets us lose sight of the human Jesus and the impact he made on his contemporaries and their expectations of his ministry. We now need to ask: How do we account, humanly speaking, for this mysterious Person?

The impact of his authority

What was he like? No description has survived. But whatever his physical appearance, there can be no doubt that he was a riveting teacher, arresting and challenging. All four Gospels speak of the huge crowds that followed him. Mark, for instance, speaks of how 'the crowds again gathered round him: and, again, as was his custom, he again taught them'. In fact, Mark emphasises how great an element in the impact Jesus had on people lay in this very public teaching and preaching, not only by the countless occasions he describes, but in Jesus' own reference to it as the soldiers arrested him in the Garden of Gethsemane: 'Day after day I sat with you, teaching in the temple courts and you did not arrest me.' Although we can be sure that Jesus himself was the greatest draw, his teaching style must have been evocative and attractive. The stories that have come down to us show how colourful was his style, rich with stories and pictures from the common life that all shared. Pictures of human relationships, domestic mishaps, concerns about crops, and anxiety about making ends meet; and awareness of the power over simple lives of great lords, kings and rich men. In addition there is the countryman's keen eye for the natural world, birds, flowers, seeds. And there are the marvellous aphorisms. All four Gospels record them. Sayings like: 'Those who want to save their lives will lose it and those who lose their life for my sake and for the sake of the gospel will save it'; or: 'With God all things are possible'; or: 'If you had faith like a mustard seed you would say to this mountain' . . .

But however attractive was Jesus' style and however vivid was his teaching, it wasn't these qualities that drew the crowds. What drew them was the most distinctive feature and quality of his teaching: its authority. Not for him the tentative, apologetic form that marked the teaching of the scribes, or even the complex arguing of the rabbis. Both Mark and Matthew record that Jesus taught 'as one having authority, and not as the scribes'.

Authority. Inevitably such authority, derived as it is from personal charisma and sources that lie outside convention, raises questions, increasingly hostile. One of the clearest pictures of Jesus in his own time is of gathering hostility from a number of quarters. From his own village: '"Where did this man get these things?" they asked. "What's this wisdom that has been given him that he even does miracles? Isn't this the carpenter? Isn't this Mary's son and the brother of James, Joseph, Judas and

Simon? Aren't his sisters here with us?" And they took offence at him' (Mark 6:2b–3). There is a familiarity about such an objection which links our day with Jesus' time; it is the vivid account of small-town prejudice against one of its number getting above himself.

But much more dangerous hostility was being aroused and it came not from those who knew Jesus best but from those who represented the powers of the establishment; the chief priests, the scribes and elders were aroused not only by his teaching but even more so by the authoritative actions that accompanied it. Nothing could more clearly have indicated Jesus' implication of his own inherent authority than in his purging of the Temple of its corrupt commercialism. All four Gospels record it and each one follows the story with the same question from outraged 'authority' represented by the men who held office. They 'came to him as he was teaching' and asked him: 'By what authority are you doing these things and who gave you that authority?'

Authority. It's there in his teaching; it's there in certain actions he takes; it's there in his healing, even of 'evil spirit possession'. Mark's first recorded miracle is in the context of a healing in the synagogue at Capernaum, where he both teaches and heals 'the man with an unclean spirit'. The marvelling crowd respond by saying: 'What is this? A new teaching with authority!' He shows authority in forgiving sins and backs it up by healing those forgiven. 'He commands even the unclean spirits, and they obey him.'

So, a Jew of his times, and yet with an inherent authority in action, word and attitude which set him over against his times. A most public figure, followed by crowds; and yet one who seems to have avoided all the major cities except Jerusalem, keeping to the small towns and villages and the desert. One who preached publicly, and yet by word and action implied claims about possessing a unique relationship with God his Father, concerning which he urged, for much of the time, silence. Time and again, for instance, he charged those he cured to secrecy, commanding them not to disclose who had healed them. Indeed, at times he seems (particularly in Mark's account) to have been keeping a 'messianic secret', not fully declaring his true identity till the time should be right. And to that right time and its connectedness to his death we shall come in due course.

Four 'channels': the same topic, different views

Until quite recently, we had in England four major TV channels, with satellite and cable pay channels multiplying rapidly. (I guess that in your day 'couch potatoes', as we call people who spend hours watching TV, will have the choice of hundreds of TV channels. A ghastly thought, I must admit!) We could draw an analogy between the operation of these four TV stations and the four Gospels I am writing about. If there's a major event these four channels will report it. But I have noticed that they will pick out different bits to emphasise, or they might even interpret the event totally differently, according to their audience and its interests or, perhaps, according to the type of 'message' they wish to get across.

Roughly, that's our experience in 'reading' the event of Jesus impacting on his society when the four different 'channels' – Mark, Matthew, Luke and John – were put together. *Mark*, for instance, was writing to a predominantly Roman world in the early 60s. His story is direct and he highlights that Jesus was urging through word and deed a way of relating to God that was not primarily through the Law but through the Father–child relationship. Mark emphasised the self-designation of Jesus as 'Son of Man', the meaning of which is still disputed. No doubt Jesus drew this partly from the book of Ezekiel where the prophet used it simply as a synonym for 'me' or 'I'. But it is thought that Jesus wanted people of his day who knew their Scriptures well to catch a hint that he was also referring to the book of Daniel where the 'Son of Man' is a messianic figure destined to be an agent of judgement. As used by Jesus the phrase conveyed a breadth of interpretation and yet remained sufficiently mysterious and cryptic so as to allow his disciples and other followers to advance in their knowledge of him.

For *Matthew*, Jesus is the great teacher and law-giver; the new Moses. He quotes Jesus as saying: 'You have heard that it was said to those of ancient times . . . *But I say to you* . . .' And what he had to say was not an abolition of the Torah, the Law, but a recovery of its original intention, the ethical expression of an attitude of mind and heart without which no amount of formal observance of the Law's demands had value. What comes authentically through Matthew is the sharp area of contention with the religious authorities, where he challenged not only their authority but also their perception of what was important about the Law.

By contrast, the *Luke* 'channel' is directed at a different audience, a non-Jewish one. So issues about the upholding of the minutiae of the Torah are not going to be the centre of Luke's interest. And yet it is the same message, differently focused; a message about how God addresses the condition of the heart. Whereas Matthew has in mind a Jewish audience, Luke's interest is the appeal of Jesus to all people in need of God's grace. Luke describes how Jesus ministered through physical, emotional and psychic acts of healing to all sorts and conditions of people, as in his meeting with the tax collector, Zacchaeus, an incident that only Luke describes. (By the term 'psychic' here I mean nothing more than 'of the soul' and am implying no approval of the practices of modern-day 'psychic-healers'.) And it is Luke who gives to us some of the most precious and priceless of Jesus' stories – parables like 'the lost coin', 'the Prodigal Son' (or as it is sometimes called 'the Loving Father'), 'the Good Samaritan', 'Dives and Lazarus'. In all this it is the grace of Jesus' message about God which is offered to all people.

So it is not a different person who is being described by Matthew and Luke. It is the same wandering teacher, speaking with extraordinary authority and performing actions which connect with that teaching and authority. Acts which suggest an authority over the physical elements of Creation, whether that of healing the human body or of satisfying hunger out of what would seem inadequate provisions. And all of these are of a piece with the God to whom Jesus is witnessing. For Matthew it is Israel's God; for Luke it is the God of the whole world.

And what of the fourth 'channel', the Gospel of *John*? What contemporary impact by Jesus do we discover in John? We have already seen that his version of the beginning is on a different plane from the other three. The strange authority which is so consistent a keynote in the Synoptic Gospels is seen by John as the 'glory' of God himself. 'The Word became flesh and made his dwelling among us. We have seen his glory, the glory of the One and Only, who came from the Father, full of grace and truth' (John 1:14). If there is one word central to John's description of the impact Jesus made on those closest to him, it is that word 'glory'. Yet this is the same wandering teacher he is talking about. What appears to be happening here is that both John's beginning and the story of Jesus he goes on to tell fuse faith-statement and history more totally than the other three. We can see this clearly enough in John's characteristic word to describe the unique quality of this Person. As Mark used the phrase 'Son of Man' to portray the mystery of Jesus, the Fourth Gospel uses the term 'Logos'. It was a word familiar in both Jewish and Gentile worlds, though no one uses it in the New Testament apart from John. It denoted an intelligent principle behind the universe and was a very popular term in the sophisticated and intelligent world of the later first century. And what John does is to adopt this term and use it in an entirely novel sense – he made it personal to Jesus, the man who lived in first-century Judaea. 'This man,' he states boldly, 'is the Logos of God who came from God and who is God.' So the prologue of John's Gospel (1:1–18) is a breathtaking statement of the divinity and humanity of this one who, though being God, became human with a humanity which shone, for those with eyes to see it, with the glory of God.

'For those with eyes to see it.' The counterpoint to John's theme of glory which shone in Jesus for those drawn to him, is his account of non-recognition by so many who could have been expected to know him. There is a deep sadness in the prologue where John records: 'He came to that which was his own, but his own did not receive him.' That sadness is known by so many Christians as we seek to communicate the glory of Jesus Christ to others, only to find that so many are strangely blind to the glory.

But what is the nature of this glory? John describes no ethereal being floating ten feet above the earth, immune and impervious to the grime, sin and suffering of wounded humanity. John, perhaps more than the other gospellers, brings home to us the real humanity of Jesus. He describes Jesus' acute weariness after a day's travel: 'Jesus, tired as he was from the journey, sat down by the well' (4:6). It is John who tells of Jesus grieving at the death of a dear friend, Lazarus. Indeed, as we shall see when I write to you about why Jesus had to die, at the heart of the sense of glory was a realisation that the only glory that really matters is the kind of living which gives itself away in suffering and death: 'Unless a grain of wheat falls to the ground and dies, it remains only a single seed. But if it dies, it produces many seeds' (12:24).

At this point I want to tell you of one of the great archbishops of this century, Michael Ramsey. I was privileged to know him in his retirement. Michael was a man whose understanding of the Christian faith was shot through with this theme of glory. No doubt many wonderful stories will have come down to your time about this remarkable servant of God. He was undoubtedly ill at ease in our media-conscious world in which the 'thirty-second sound byte' counts for more than serious debate and search for truth. But once Michael was in a pulpit or lecture room talking about Jesus, the glory he was zealous to impart seemed to transfigure Michael himself. His words would have a searing magic, his demeanour a great authority, and his argument would be compelling and majestic. Indeed, Michael himself was an epitome of the great truth that those who belong to Christ share in the glory of Christ. He wrote: 'Beneath every act in the Church whereby this many-sided work of glory is being wrought, there is a truth about the Church's essential being, namely that the glory of Christ is *there*. The glory which Christians are to grow into and to manifest by their practical response of the Christian life is a glory which is *theirs* already.'

To return to John's Gospel: just as the Jesus John describes carries glory with him inextinguishably, so this Jesus is open about who he is. There are no 'messianic secrets' for the people John's Gospel represents. The Jesus of John not only knows who he is, he is prepared to talk about it and demonstrate it.

This shows in the way the Gospel of John was written. In his account of the miracles, for instance. John seems to have been deliberately selective in his description of Jesus' miracles, mentioning only seven. The important thing about this is that they are all called 'signs' – they are direct testimonies to that same glory. And his teaching follows the same pattern. It is gathered into seven great chunks – 'discourses' as they are usually described – grouped round seven pictures or images by which the Fourth Gospel captured the glory of the Person of Jesus: 'I am the bread of life . . . I am the true vine . . . I am the Good Shepherd . . . I am the Light of the world' and so on. These are clear – and as a consequence, to those who did not recognise him, blasphemous – parallels to the 'I AM's of the Old Testament. Indeed, John's Gospel brings vividly alive the controversy that Jesus aroused in his day. For example, John reports that Jesus claimed: 'Before Abraham was born, I am' (8:58).

Those faced with such a claim had no middle course; this man was either mad or blasphemous, or he was speaking plain truth. So by his words as well as by his actions Jesus' impact on those he met was to push them to a choice. And the condition of that choice was to recognise what sort of God was actually theirs and to discover by seeing God in Jesus that they were actually meeting him for the first time. So Philip said: '"Lord, show us the

Father and that will be enough for us." Jesus answered: "Don't you know me, Philip, even after I have been among you such a long time? Anyone who has seen me has seen the Father"' (14:8–9).

And what kind of Father and what kind of Son? The kind whose quality of authority, leadership and power was demonstrated by washing his followers' feet and by undertaking the slave's task of serving. It is that kind of self-giving through which the true nature of glory is revealed.

Recognising Jesus: Caesarea Philippi

The moment came when recognition dawned on those who had become closest to him, as they followed him about the villages and small towns and deserts of Judaea. They began to see him in a different light as an awareness of his difference from them became an awesome reality. This moment of recognition is important to our recovering the Jesus of his times, not least because it took place during his ministry, not after the great moments such as Good Friday, Easter and Pentecost. And clearly his followers, looking back, saw it as one of the key moments of his time with them. For all four Gospels record it, though John very obliquely.

Now it is worth noting the different way they tell it: the differences belong to the specific message that each Evangelist wants to communicate about Jesus.

Mark's account is very brief. It goes like this: Jesus is asking, as they approach Caesarea Philippi, what the word is on the street about him. Their reply runs with what we've already noted about Mark's concerns: the general opinion is that he is a messenger sent from God – Elijah or even the now-executed John the Baptist. The categories are of one bringing a warning of judgement. Then Jesus turns the question away from the comfortable gossip of other people's opinions to what the disciples themselves believe. Jesus' real interest is now revealed: do his own disciples really know *who* he is? Peter's reply shows how far he has travelled: 'You are the Christ' (Mark 8:29). The statement of recognition Peter makes is his own, but it is also on behalf of them all. This is the Coming One; God's own Deliverer who walks this dusty road with them.

And that is all Mark tells us; no commendation of Peter's faith, no development of the implications. Only the sharp command to secrecy: 'And he sternly ordered them not to tell anyone about him.' The 'messianic secret' remains, but it is now one the disciples have discovered together.

If we turn to *Matthew's* version the core of the incident remains intact, just as Mark told it, but Matthew is one for whom the implications of the future of God's people are important. We pick up the same story at Jesus' question to them: 'Who do you say I am?' The disciples are thus pushed to make an open acknowledgement and Peter says it for them: 'You are the Christ, the Son of the living God.' And Jesus, in Matthew, sees Peter as central to the new structure that will express the rule of God on earth. Hence the importance to Matthew of Jesus' commendation: 'Blessed are you, Simon son of Jonah . . . And I tell you that you are Peter, and on this rock I will build my church.' Here for the first time we meet the concept of a 'church' which will emerge from faith in Christ.

This prophecy is not followed up, as in Mark, by the stern injunction to secrecy but by a comment on the source of their perception. Their understanding of who and what their enigmatic leader is, as expressed by Peter,

has been given to them not through natural understanding but as a direct gift from God the Father: 'For this
was not revealed to you by man, but by my Father in
heaven.'

Luke's emphases are subtly different again. He echoes
Matthew's version very largely, but the context he gives is
not that of wayside conversation but of prayer. And then,
following Mark, he relays Christ's injunction to secrecy:
'Jesus strictly ordered them not to tell this to anyone.'

Why, incidentally, this tremendously stern warning to
keep the secret? We live in a media age, and perhaps that
helps us better to understand what Jesus was anxious to
avoid – that is, the way talk *about* something can affect the
substance of what is being communicated. Even though
Jesus has disclosed himself as the Christ to his disciples,
the full content of what that meant had to await the Cross
and Resurrection.

And so we come to *John's* very oblique reference to this
incident (6:60–71). It is stripped of all its topographical
detail and placed in the context of something that certainly was to happen – the falling away of many who had
begun to follow him with enthusiasm. They complain:
'This is a hard teaching. Who can accept it?' and 'many of
his disciples turned back and no longer followed him'. It
is another glimpse of the Jesus his contemporaries knew;
the uncompromising Jesus who would not modify his
message to retain his following (we in the Church might
well take note!). However, there is something very
poignant in Jesus' question to the Twelve: 'You do not
want to leave too, do you?' Peter's response to Jesus' ter-
ribly sad question is a response that comes from profound
recognition of Jesus: 'Lord, to whom shall we go? You
have the words of eternal life. We believe and know that
you are the Holy One of God.'

Jesus – back to the beginning

So, in sum, who and what did his contemporaries experience when they met Jesus? We do not need to be agnostic about this. A figure is visible and comes to us freshly through the pages of the New Testament. They met someone who was a recognisable figure of his time, with a known family and home town, who gave up a job he was known for (carpentry) and became another kind of familiar figure of his time, a wandering teacher.

But we can say much more than that. At points in his ministry this teacher attracted great crowds. He was compellingly magnetic and spoke with an authority which was overwhelmingly real – but puzzling. He addressed the disturbed but expectant state of the nation on the very issues it yearned over, but his teaching was disconcertingly opaque and elusive. It is most unlikely that he thought or implied that the end of the world was near. The apocalyptic language he used was common at the time and it gave him scope to talk of God's judgement and salvation without giving a time and date to the coming of God. There were times when he was stern. Hypocrisy was something he especially condemned and the religious authorities often came under the piercing analysis of his teaching. His followers too were not exempt from his rebuke when their concern for others fell below the standards of his love.

But above all he was compassionate and effective in his compassion. The gospel story abounds in descriptions of his tender love for the outcast and the down-trodden, as well as for ordinary people who were drawn to a religious teacher whose love for the natural world connected with their own. He wined and dined with them to the extent that he was accused of having too good a time with them.

'Celebration', in other words, was not alien to this man who showed what God was like. He taught them of a Father God who was faithful to his people Israel. He taught that knowing and loving the Father God was like a great pearl or a treasure in a field and one must make it one's heart's desire. For that same God was such that he would seek out the lost and longing and bring them home; like a shepherd with lost sheep, like a father with a lost son, like a woman with a lost coin. And such a God rejoiced over all the lost who were found.

And such a God was about to usher in his kingdom, and through his elusive teaching Jesus signalled that his death as well as his life was instrumental in bringing this about.

This, then, was the Jesus whom his contemporaries met. I hope it thrills you as much as it still thrills me after so many years of studying him. And yet his contemporaries were going to be even more amazed by him in the end. And that will be the content of my next Letter.

Yours in thankfulness for the Jesus of history,

George

LETTER 7

The Resurrection of Jesus Christ

Dear Friends of the Future,

I recently visited one of our theological colleges. It was vibratingly alive with some splendid men and women in training who continue to come forward, in spite of all the ups and downs of the Church, to offer themselves to God. We are currently looking hard at our training to see if we can do it better, and some very exciting developments in theological education are emerging. Nevertheless, I believe that my generation – and yours – must continue to remember that prior to everything to do with structures, management, policy and finances, is the bedrock of Christian assurance. For myself, as a former College Principal, I remain convinced that above all else the training must take the student more deeply and challengingly into relationship with Jesus and must lead to a profounder and more mature grasp of the faith. Otherwise the whizz-kids we may create – while knowing all about information technology and all the specialisms of ministry – may have little to offer the faith-needs of our world; or yours.

I enjoyed talking with the students and gleaned many valuable things from them about their training. Most of all I found that what excited them was the very thing that excited me when I started out as a struggling disciple of our Lord so many years ago. So I shared with them what I regard as the most important insight any Christian could possibly have.

The most important insight of all

'What is it?' I can almost hear you asking! Well, I remember studying the Acts of the Apostles as a student and I suddenly found myself asking: 'Why didn't the earliest preaching say something more about the meaning of the death of Jesus?' I couldn't understand why the apostles did not explain more what it meant.

As I thought about this puzzle I was led to understand something very important which conveyed a real ring of truth: if I had been there, what would I have preached? Suddenly the penny dropped. 'The Resurrection, of course!' For men and women who had seen Jesus captured and killed, who had helped to bury him, the staggering and stunning experience was that Jesus was alive. 'God has made this Jesus, whom you crucified, both Lord and Christ' (Acts 2:36). So they preached. Not at this point a great theology of the Cross; that was to come later. The record of the early preaching in Acts shows again and again the priority of the Resurrection above all else. The apostles 'continued to testify to the resurrection of the Lord Jesus, and much grace was upon them all' (Acts 4:33).

In my earlier Letters to you we set out to discover how Jesus was known in his own time. We saw that in spite of the later speculations of the Church and indeed the hindsight of the disciples, a real, exciting and believable Person emerges from the pages of the New Testament. And, of course, at the end of those brief three years the next thing that happened was his death. So, chronologically, that is what we should be looking at next. But there are acute difficulties with that. You see, the meaning and the necessity of Jesus' death was only something the disciples began to understand much later on. That is to say, when they had looked at it through the lens of the Resurrection. They had to go through the terrible experiences we commemorate on Good Friday without any sense of – or hope for – what we celebrate on Easter Day. For them the death of Jesus was not glimpsed as a victory over sin. Quite the reverse. For them it was total and annihilating defeat for their Master and total bereavement for themselves as a group. They saw him die and with him died all the hopes that had grown during the thrilling three years of ministry. As one of them put it to that 'Stranger' on the Emmaus Road: 'The chief priests and our rulers handed him over to be sentenced to death, and they crucified him; but we had hoped that he was the one who was going to redeem Israel' (Luke 24:21).

So what they saw at the Cross was, starkly, a death; an appalling, shameful death of the most humiliating kind. What they saw and experienced *next* was the event that reshaped, charged and totally changed their understanding not only of Jesus' death but of all that had gone before. What they saw was their Lord, their friend and Lord Jesus, alive. Alive beyond death, alive and with them in a wholly recognisable form that was utterly 'him' and yet materially different in that doors, walls, space and time were no barriers to this glorified humanity. They saw Jesus alive, vividly alive, after that terrible and unforgettable death.

So it was this that was the most important truth of all. Of course they did not preach the Cross at this point. There was nothing unique about dying on a cross; right across the territories ruled by Rome the whole population lived in the shadow of crosses and gibbets. Nothing unique, either, in being crucified unjustly as a young, charismatic leader of men. But what was unique was for that young leader to return from death, victorious over that death which they had most certainly seen him die. So, naturally, the early Church preached the Resurrection, the risen Christ; and it was in the extraordinary power of that truth that the young Church's astonishing vitality was rooted.

What it means to say that Jesus is alive

So the Resurrection is the root centre of Christianity. 'Jesus lives!' is the radical truth with implications for everyone and every situation. The Resurrection is the fact which makes Christianity a faith. For the Resurrection interprets everything, as our own Doctrine Commission pointed out quite recently: 'The life of Christ, the death of Christ, the relationship of God with his people throughout history, the personal life of every believer, the future of the Church, and the potential and hope of the entire cosmos itself.'

So the Resurrection is not a happy ending to the story of Jesus. Much more than an ending, it is a beginning. The beginning for us all of the new life in Christ. It is this event which interprets the whole Bible and especially the New Testament. Throughout the New Testament it is the risen Christ who is its impressive centre.

I hope you can see now why in this Letter, before we turn to the great and terrible truths of the Cross, we must make a journey of discovery with the first disciples to the mystery of the Resurrection. The Gospels themselves were written after the Resurrection by men quite sure of its reality. We begin, however, with the testimony of Paul – for the very good reason that his testimony comes first.

Paul and the risen Jesus

In 1 Corinthians 15, written AD 54, Paul gives his own testimony about the Resurrection. He was a converted Jewish rabbi, a highly intelligent, sophisticatedly educated, subtle, resourceful man. He cannot be seen as a credulous would-be believer. Even if he had been yearning to believe in something other than Judaism, as a rabbinically trained man he would have found the crucifixion and claims of a resurrection huge stumbling-blocks to faith. There is absolutely no evidence, either from himself or others, that he had any desire whatever to take up the cause of this new claimant to messiahship. Quite the reverse. He saw it as an obnoxious and blasphemous faith which must be rooted out. So something quite astounding happened to him; an event which turned upside-down his whole view of the new faith; turning this persecutor of Christians into one compelled by the fact of the Resurrection to blaze it forth across the then civilised world.

Paul tells us what happened: 'Last of all he appeared to me also, as to one abnormally born' (1 Corinthians 15:8). He sees this as an all-important element in his commissioning to preach the faith. That is, what mattered was not whether he had shared with the apostles Jesus' ministry, or had been present with them at the crucifixion: no, what mattered was that he had shared their direct experience of the risen Christ. Nothing could more strikingly attest the overwhelming importance of the Resurrection to that young Church. Paul was not reasoned into faith in the risen Christ; he met him on the road to Damascus. And that for Paul, and for the Church, was enough.

And yet Paul is quite clear that this was the last 'resurrection' appearance. The risen Christ will indeed be known to those who are to come, but in other ways, facilitated by the Holy Spirit, sometimes directly, and at other times indirectly through the Church, the body of Christ. Therefore, Paul's calling was so to present the faith that men and women who will never meet Christ in such a tangible form may now 'meet' and encounter him in their hearts and experience for themselves that Jesus is alive!

Presenting the evidence

Four different types of evidence for the resurrection of Jesus are presented in 1 Corinthians 15. These are inherent in Paul's account that:

• Christ died for our sins according to Scripture.

• He was buried.

• He was raised on the third day.

• He appeared to Peter, to the Twelve, to 500, to James and, last of all, to Paul.

We can see at once that different kinds of evidence are posited here. Paul is saying that Scripture had foretold the coming of the Messiah; that the fact of the missing body had to be explained; that an overwhelming number of people had met the risen Christ; and, finally, and most crucially to Paul, he himself had met the risen Christ and had spoken to him. So absolute had been this experience that it had wholly changed his life. Let us look more closely at these different kinds of evidence.

The testimony of Scripture and the faith community

To our eyes the Old Testament – 'Scripture' in Paul's meaning of the word – says very little about the death and resurrection of Jesus. But this was not how the first Christians saw it. From the very beginning the first disciples, brought up in the Jewish faith, saw hints of the story of Jesus in such passages of the Old Testament as the vision of Daniel's Son of Man; in Isaiah's Suffering Servant; in the book of Proverbs' Wisdom figure; in Jeremiah's New Covenant and in many other places.

Coming at this cold it seems pretty tenuous stuff. Picking out individual verses in a highly selective manner is no way to do justice to the Old Testament. That way, we would think, you can prove anything. But, of course, those early Christians were *not* 'coming at them cold'. They were coming to them in two interpretative and empowering contexts.

First, in the context of the Jewish faith and the worshipping community in which they had been reared. This was a context of longing and hope. Jews were brought up to expect the coming of the Messiah; one who would usher in the kingdom of God. They consequently interpreted the Scriptures messianically. It is hardly surprising that the first Christians did the same and found them redolent with clues about Christ.

The second context was in their encounter with Christ himself, either in the flesh or, in the days of the early Church, through the community of believers. In his earthly ministry Jesus had made his followers understand the Scriptures messianically. He suggested in his preaching that the Old Testament spoke of him. He brought the past, the present and the future together in such a way that people saw him as the fulfilment of Scriptural prophecy. As Peter proclaimed on the Day of Pentecost, 'this Jesus' was the figure in whom all the allusive hints of Scripture came together. Thus, naturally, books of proof texts arose in the early Church to show that Jesus' death and resurrection were in conformity with Old Testament expectation.

There is a truth here of the greatest importance for your generation as it is for mine. That is, resurrection belief is only fully entered into in the context of the faith life of the community of believers. It is neither an intellectual concept to be reached by cold and lonely logic, nor a subjective experience so highly individual as to be opaque to everyone else. The authentic experience of the reality that Jesus is alive may for most of us only be fully seized as we participate in the faith life of fellow Christians. One of the greatest English theologians of my time, Dr Austin Farrer, put it memorably in this way:

> What Christians find in Christ through faith inclines them at certain points to accept with regard to him testimony about matters of fact which would be inconclusive if offered with regard to any other man . . . Thus it is possible, through faith and evidence together, and through neither alone, to believe that Christ really and corporeally rose from the dead, not merely that his death on the cross had a supernatural silver lining significant for our salvation. Obviously the use of faith to confirm evidence makes the most exacting demands on intellectual honesty. We must believe neither without evidence nor against evidence.

Jesus died and was buried. This takes us to the evidence of the material – the physical – facts. The honest enquirer deeply interested in what happened to Jesus is faced with two *certain* facts. Jesus was crucified and so died. And he was buried. Some have speculated that he merely swooned on the Cross and was taken down supposedly dead, later recovered in the tomb, and staggered away from the tomb to friends. This is frankly utterly implausible, not least because it is highly unlikely that any self-respecting Roman soldier would have been taken in by a swoon (we must remember that there was nothing exceptional or unusual about such executions as part of the routine duty for soldiers). Further, it requires us to believe that a dreadfully injured person would have the strength to take the burial clothes from his body and move the stone at the mouth of the tomb – a stone large enough to deter strong grave robbers from plundering it. Moreover it is not credible in relation to the Jesus we have met during his ministry that he would lend himself to the fiction that he had been dead but was 'raised' by God for his divine purposes. The whole point about Jesus, throughout his ministry, is that only the truth will do. And indeed, the Jesus we have known in his ministry had set his face like flint towards death. He was 'absolute for death' in Stevie Smith's powerful phrase.

There is another hypothesis we must refute. It states that it is not uncommon for people who passionately want to believe something to be so convinced that the wish becomes translated into 'reality' for them. So the Resurrection happened because the disciples wanted it to happen. This too is unconvincing because the Gospels make it clear that the disciples had no notion at all of such a thing happening. There is no wistful hope, no tentative speculation in the Gospels. He is dead, and they, and the womenfolk with them, are in profound grief at their loss, mixed with great fear of the authorities. What rings true in the records is that Jesus tried to prepare them for both the grief that awaited them, and for the hope beyond that, yet they seemed unable to assimilate either. It was only with hindsight, after the shock of his death and the amazement of his raising, that they looked back and remembered his words and at last understood his meaning.

Both theories are pretty desperate attempts to make sense of these two important material facts: Jesus died; his body disappeared. I am writing this during a week when our papers are full of a murder trial. The accused man had murdered his wife, but after the deed he realised that he had to remove all evidence. He decided to dissect the body and then cooked it and diced it. But even this barbaric solution did not work because, as he found out to his cost, it is most difficult to make a body vanish. To such physical realities we must add the political reality that the search for Christ's missing body when claims of his resurrection began would have been intensive, and backed, one imagines, by both threat and bribery. All the authorities had to do was to produce the body. But the tomb was empty. And those whose cause was served by this -- the disciples -- were as openly astonished as everyone else. Professor Geza Vermes, writing from a strictly Jewish and historical perspective some years back, looked exhaustively at the evidence and concluded:

> In the end, when every argument has been considered and weighed, the only conclusion acceptable to the historian must be that the opinions of the orthodox, the liberal sympathiser and critical agnostic alike ... are strictly interpretations of the one disconcerting fact; namely, that the women who set out to pay their last respects to Jesus found to their consternation, not a body, but an empty tomb.

The disconcerting fact. Jesus had been placed in the tomb and yet the tomb was empty.

But that on its own did not create the Christian faith. Mary Magdalene, the first to discover the empty tomb, did not – at all – leap to the conclusion that her beloved Master was 'risen'. Far from it. Her immediate assumption was that Jesus' body had been stolen, or at least moved. And so she said to the one she thought was the gardener, 'Tell me where he has been laid.' An empty tomb of itself did not imply a living Lord.

Moreover, we should note the fact that the disciples were in no position to capitalise on it, unsupported by other evidence that Jesus was alive. They were not expecting the Resurrection; they were not only grieving but they were terrified for their own safety. They had fled in disorder and when they gathered together again it was behind locked doors because of their fear. It is inconceivable that this grieving, frightened huddle could steal the body, hide it, and then be so lit with a passionate confidence that they fearlessly began to preach a gospel about the *truth* of the victorious love of God, seen in a risen Lord. A missing body only proves that a body went missing. It doesn't transform a terrified huddle into a joyful and courageous group who take their stand on the truth of what they have seen in Jesus.

So, to the mystery of the empty tomb we have to add the mystery of the transformation of the disciples. Both these were objective, observable facts: the tomb was empty and the disciples were utterly changed people.

The evidence of the witnesses

And that leads us directly on to what so many witnesses claim to have seen. Paul, writing to Corinth some twenty years later, can state as uncontested fact that Jesus 'was raised on the third day . . . he appeared to Peter, and then to the Twelve. After that he appeared to more than five hundred of the brothers at the same time . . . and last of all he appeared to me'. It is an impressive list, and to it we must add the testimony of the four Gospels which, written later than this epistle, also give evidence of witnesses to the risen Christ.

But, it can be rightly argued, there are differences in the resurrection accounts of the Gospels; does not this challenge the authenticity of the story? Mark, for example, has a broken ending with the Gospel left unfinished; the keynote of that unfinished ending is terrified amazement (16:8), and a strong measure of disbelief. There is disagreement too between the Gospels as to who was there at the tomb when Mary came early in the morning. Mark speaks of a 'young man dressed in a white robe', Luke describes 'two men in clothes that gleamed like lightning', Matthew speaks of 'an angel . . . His appearance was like lightning, and his clothes were white as snow'. As for John, he describes 'two angels in white'. There are similar divergences between the Gospels in their account of the resurrection appearances and in their emphases as they recount these.

Yet, even with respect to the examples I have given, there is sufficient convergence to inspire confidence. Clearly 'someone' (or two) was there, was dressed in white that shone or dazzled, and spoke authoritatively of Jesus himself. Anyone who has listened to four versions of the same incident will find such discrepancies exactly the sort that creep into accounts from different viewers. Clearly the stories have not been standardised, so we get the almost invariable element of difference on minor details among witnesses.

More impressive than the disparities are the similarities. The Gospels agree that Jesus was dead and buried/the disciples were not prepared for his death and fled in confusion/none of them expected his raising to life/the tomb on Easter morning was empty/Mary Magdalene was the first witness/there were many accounts of Jesus appearing to his followers/the Resurrection was proclaimed in Jerusalem – the very place where hundreds had seen him put to death. They knew for a fact that he was dead.

To these we have to add the account Paul gives of Jesus' 'resurrection appearance' to himself. There is the same quality of unexpectedness, of dazzle, of awe and wonder – and, above all else, a sense of the reality that a life is changed for ever, for it is now understood differently. There is too the same sense of utter authority. We may compare it with Thomas' reaction 'My Lord and my God!' (John 20:28); or with the disciples' reaction to the miraculous draft of fish at day-break by the sea of Tiberias; or with the recognition at the breaking of bread by those who had walked with him on the Emmaus Road.

What was the mode of the Resurrection?

So we are led to ask: What kind of resurrection are we talking about? Since 'resurrection' collides with our human experience of death – dead men are not known to live again – there are those who seek refuge in other interpretations of the resurrection event to avoid its downright embarrassment.

Let us look at some of the interpretations. For example, some thinkers have concluded that what we know for certain is that the Church 'rose' that day. Something happened that launched the Christian faith. So, it is argued, since the disciples experienced 'something' – of that there can be no doubt – we need not worry overmuch about the content of that experience. *They* came alive and that is a cause of profound thanksgiving. This approach does highlight what we have already noted as a matter of great importance: the change in the disciples. Indeed, I want to return to that later. Nevertheless, the argument itself is decidedly unconvincing. It entails that the disciples who had shown such terror and had fled from the scene of crucifixion were now radiant disciples willing to face death themselves, not because they had witnessed a *real* event which had changed their whole mindset, but because they *felt* as though he had been raised from the dead. We do not need training in psychology to know that an experience grounded in wishful thinking will not stand up to the harsh tests of reality – to which, in this case, they were rapidly exposed.

Another approach akin to this is the denial of the physical nature of the Resurrection. There are scholars – and reputable ones at that – who believe that the Resurrection should be understood in *spiritual* terms only. This, they argue, is real enough indeed because the 'spirit' of Jesus lives on in the world through his followers in his living Church. They claim, furthermore, that Christianity would be more sympathetically received if it surrendered its emphasis on the bodily resurrection of Christ.

It is important for us to listen to the New Testament and to hear what it is actually saying. It states that **the Resurrection of Jesus was of the same order of reality as his death: he died and he rose**. That is to say that though no longer subject to the constraints of space and time, yet it was in the physical body, with the marks of the wounds on it, that Jesus appeared to his disciples. Paul stated that according to the tradition he received, Christ was buried. Why should he go out of his way to say so obvious a thing? Because he is obliquely mentioning the empty tomb, and doing so to a group who, it becomes clear, want to spiritualise the Resurrection. Paul is therefore indirectly insisting that the entombed body of Jesus is the risen body of Jesus. John 20 similarly recalls that the risen Christ invited Thomas to put his finger in the marks made by the nails and his hand in Jesus' side. Luke's Gospel is making the same point about the physical nature of the body of the risen Lord when it describes how, at his first appearing to his disciples, he is insistent that he is no 'spirit'. 'Look at my hands and my feet. It is I myself! Touch me and see' (Luke 24:39, 41b–43).

Of course, the risen body of Jesus transcends his physical nature. We saw earlier that his body was physical yet transformed. It was not bound by material and spatial limits. Tantalisingly the Gospels show that Jesus could materialise at will and transcend localisation. (In a real way, we might reverently assume, the resurrection body of Christ anticipates the resurrection body of every Christian; there is identity and yet difference. We shall consider this later.)

What is clear from all this is that the New Testament gives us no grounds for believing that the Resurrection was 'spiritual' only. It was a resurrection of the whole person, spiritual and physical. The risen body of Jesus was that which had been crucified and laid to rest. No other interpretation will do, or will satisfy the demands of the Biblical text. It was, after all, the marks of the nails in the hands of Jesus which convinced Thomas.

Some circumstantial evidence

To all the above we need to add some circumstantial evidence. First, there was the change in the day Christians marked as the day of rest. Very quickly the young Church

abandoned the Jewish Shabbat – worship on the seventh
day. Considering the importance of the Old Testament to
the first Christians, this departure is a very remarkable
fact. But from their very beginning as a faith group the
Christians gathered for worship on the *first* day of the
week. Only something very significant could have led
devout Jews (as they were) to make so dramatic a change.
The Gospels tell us what that reason was: 'On the first day
of the week, just after sunrise, they were on their way to
the tomb' (Mark 16:2). The Christian Church continues
this practice each week as we worship on the first day.
This itself is a statement that Jesus is alive.

But of course the most powerful circumstantial evidence of all is in the continued transformation of the disciples. No clever trickery on their part could have
changed those who 'forsook him and fled', who began to
curse and swear 'I do not know the man,' who met after
his death 'behind locked doors'. No body-stealing, no
patching up of a badly wounded and defeated leader, no
political manoeuvring, or even a thoughtful remember-
ing of a great teacher – none of these could have changed
them so completely and for ever that when the authorities
had seen 'the courage of Peter and John' they recognised
in them the living quality of Jesus (Acts 4:13).

In other words, they were alive with the life, the risen
life of Jesus. And so we move from evidence to meaning.
What does the Resurrection *mean* for us?

The meaning of the Resurrection

At the beginning of this Letter I summed up what the
Resurrection 'meant'. I said that it interpreted everything:
the life of Christ, the death of Christ, the relationship of
God with his people throughout history, the personal life

and hope of heaven of every believer, the life and hope of the community of faith – and the hope of the very cosmos itself. Let's look at the substance of this hope now, for it is the very stuff of life for everything and everybody in your generation, as indeed in mine.

The risen Christ is Lord and Saviour

This, in fact, is what Peter preached in his first sermon as the Church was born on the Day of Pentecost: 'God has raised this Jesus to life . . . let all Israel be assured of this: God has made this Jesus, whom you crucified, both Lord and Christ' (Acts 2:32, 36).

The essential point here is the continuity between Christ's death and his Resurrection. The Resurrection declares that he is the Son of God; it witnesses to the truth of his claim. But the death of Jesus is part of that same witness. It was no accident on the way to glory but God's chosen way by which the power of sin could be broken and the awful finality of mortality dissolved. You see, we must resist the temptation to see the Resurrection on its own. To disconnect it from the work and suffering Jesus shared with humanity treats it as a divine stunt, a spectacular conjuring trick. No. The transfigured Christ of the Resurrection is actually one with, the same Person as, the disfigured Christ of the Cross. Thus, the wounded hands and feet of the risen Christ are the signs of the profound continuity between the burdened and sin-shadowed life of humanity, which Jesus embraced and took upon himself, and the hope of heaven of which he is its gate of glory. He is Lord of all; the raising up of Christ blazons forth its victory which is continuous with the victory of the Cross. So, as Helen Oppenheimer says graphically: 'The rising of Christ . . . is the pledge that the dereliction which is at the heart of Christianity – because it is at the very heart of human life – "is not the last word".'

The corollary is no less important. For the fact that Jesus lives brings home to all that God is no longer a distant unknown deity but someone whose beauty, glory and wonder are revealed through Jesus himself. To know Jesus is to know the Father; and the Resurrection assures us of our entry through the Son into the timeless life of God.

The risen Christ is 'Second Adam'

I read some sobering information the other day. A recent survey indicated that among the general public only 42 per cent believed in any destiny beyond death; and even among churchgoers only 69 per cent. This is puzzling indeed as surveys reveal that over 70 per cent of the general population claim to believe in God! Perhaps, my dear friends of the future, your generation, particularly those who share the Christian faith, will have recovered what my generation has lost: that marvellous certainty of the defeat of mortality which flows from the truth that Jesus lives. For the mystery and the marvel which touches every one of us is that since Jesus broke the power of death, it is promised that death is not the end because Jesus died to give us life.

A 'picture' way of putting this came from St Paul. The story of Adam, he reminds us, is about how humanity's relationship with God is a fractured one. Deep in the heart of every human person there is an awareness that we are all sinful sufferers, vulnerable to an awful decline into darkness of the heart and mortality of the body. Adam is the picture of this; he expresses human wilfulness – that choosing of evil in defiance of God.

Then, says Paul, see Christ as the Second Adam, reversing precisely all the evil and wretchedness focused on the first Adam. See him as renewing human obedience to God; see him as a consequence breaking the power of the way we chose, the way of evil; see him, as a further consequence, dissolving the awful grip of ultimate mortality that blocks human destiny.

One aspect of this that speaks to my generation is its holistic understanding in which body, mind and spirit are interconnected. Some have suggested very reasonably that this gives a clue as to the nature of our own life beyond death. Given the psychosomatic unity of the human being, they say, it is possible to think of the soul as the information-bearing pattern of the body. So when death dissolves the physical embodiment of the pattern, the person whose pattern that is will still be 'remembered' by God and held by him and re-embodied by him. This is, of course, only a 'picture' way of speaking and perhaps only understandable in a computer age which is also holistic in its understanding of human nature!

Let us stay with this thought. More widely there is our late-acquired awareness that decisions which concern moral and spiritual values have individual and yet global and even cosmic consequences. By your day the realities of that for our earth's good or ill will have shown themselves – I fear and strongly suspect – all too clearly.

And all this lies behind another cluster of images that Paul uses when talking about Jesus as the Second Adam. These are about Creation in relation to the human family. In Paul's thought the Creation of the universe was God's gift, effected through his power. But it is *precisely the same order of power* which effected the resurrection of Christ. Through that victory over death the very principle of 'death as the end' for us, for the globe and for the cosmos has been wiped out. The Bible refers to death as the 'last enemy' which will be overcome by Christ.

And the reality of that is with us now, though the effects of it are a matter of faith. We are already a 'new creation' in Christ. C. S. Lewis puts it simply and beautifully: 'He has forced open a door that has been locked since the death of the first man. He has met, fought and beaten the King of Death. Everything is different because he has done so.'

And that is why, of all the Letters I have written to you, dear fellow Christians of the future, this is the one I most long for you to ponder and reflect on. For here is the basis of it all, the very stuff that holds us together and enables us to speak with such certainty to generations whose whole way of life and style of civilisation may well, at the present rate of change, be wholly different from mine. In the end – literally! – the Resurrection bonds us, for we taste its present reality in each succeeding generation. And so it is from its present reality in my day that I speak to its present reality in yours.

In the risen Christ the future is anticipated

The New Testament separates history into two broad sweeps of time: this age and that to come. This age is the age of human history, dominated by man's sin and evil, and it is under 'the god of this age' (2 Corinthians 4:4). Yet the hope of the 'age to come' throbs throughout the Scriptures, not as wishful thinking but as a certainty anticipated and made available through Jesus who is alive. It is the death–resurrection event of Jesus which is the bridge between the two ages. This glorious fact makes present the benefits and the power of the new life hidden in Christ. Thus, although it is quite proper to speak of Christ's second coming in glory we should never think of this as an entirely future event. For the Christian the 'new age' has dawned in Christ and the sting of death has been drawn. It is not at all surprising, therefore, that Paul in prison facing an uncertain future could say simply and with full conviction: 'For to me, to live is Christ and to die is gain' (Philippians 1:21).

The Resurrection, therefore, not only effects the dissolving of the grip of mortality and sin on all life, but in itself anticipates the general resurrection at the Last Day. In a later Letter I shall be writing about this, but for now I simply want to say that, while we have to remain reverently agnostic about the full nature of that wonderful 'day', Scripture does assure us that the resurrection body of Christ is the pattern of our existence in God. So, St John writing to Christians towards the end of the first century puts it in a way that has never been bettered: 'What we will be has not yet been made known. But we know that when he appears, we shall be like him, for we shall see him as he is' (1 John 3:2).

The risen Christ gives people power to live new lives

My predecessor, Michael Ramsey, once recounted a surprising start to a lecture when he was a student at Cambridge attending a course on the Theology and Ethics of the New Testament. The lecturer, Sir Edwyn Hoskyns, began with the comment that the proper starting point was the Resurrection of Jesus. Michael Ramsey confessed that he was amazed, perhaps even sceptical. Surely, he thought, one begins from the *ministry* of Jesus. But as he listened his whole perception changed. Later he recorded: 'The resurrection is the true starting point for the study of the meaning of the New Testament.' And for him that meant all that the New Testament had to give in directing us in the way we should live. Michael Ramsey saw clearly that the Resurrection had the profoundest implications for those who submitted to the claims of Jesus Christ. For the disciples who first followed Jesus it meant submitting to the lordship of Christ in their daily lives. Because he was alive, their lives were under new management. Pictures such as 'taking up the Cross and following' or 'being born again' are used in the Gospels to suggest the quality of living that flows for all believers from the fact that Jesus lives. We have, indeed, 'to die' to waywardness, sin, the old life (we saw earlier that you can't have resurrection *without* death – it would be meaningless). But we live a new life empowered – precisely empowered – by the same power that raised Jesus from the grave. In the New Testament this gives rise to a new theology and a new experience of the Holy Spirit, who in a real though unspecified sense is the Spirit of Jesus. This power that indwells us is the same order of power which went into Creation, which went into the defeat of the awful power of death and which raised Jesus from the dead. That same power is made available to you and me to make us live the kind of life that honours the King of kings. St Paul describes it like this: 'I have been crucified with Christ and I no longer live, but Christ lives in me' (Galatians 2:20). This is the essence of Christian life and Christian faith.

And so, the risen Christ for those students in training . . .

Back to those students in that theological college I began with. I won't tell you which one, but they will be the seniors, in age and possibly responsibility, in the Church that you, my friends of the future, belong to. What do I hope that they will be sharing with you? Well, no doubt there will be much to keep them busy – the structures of the Church, the weary business of meetings, synods, ecumenical matters and so on and so forth. Worthy and important matters, of course. But I hope, passionately hope, that that won't dominate their faith, preaching and life! For the dynamo of the Christian life is that Jesus is risen. For if it is not true, then, as Paul said so plainly, all Christian preaching is pure folly, Christian believing is futile and Christian living is stupid and pitiable. If there were no Resurrection of Jesus then we are, as Paul put it, of all people most miserable.

And that is why I have spent so long sharing with you, of those things we have most surely believed and which have sustained us through the terrors and cynicisms of this century, this all-important shining truth – that Jesus lives. For the sturdy faith of the New Testament compels us, as I hope it will compel you, to consider again the impressive conviction of those first Christians who proclaimed the Resurrection everywhere. Its power and life will always be the hallmark of the churches and individual Christians who have really known the risen Lord. The clear message of Christianity – I sincerely hope these present students, your own future leaders, will say – is that Jesus is alive and he wants his people and his Church to be alive too.

Your devoted friend in the wonder of that message,

LETTER 8

The Young Hero Suffers and Dies

Dear Friends of the Future,

And now we come to the most painful – and yet the most powerful – truth of our faith. In my last Letter to you I was revelling in the wonder and joy of the Resurrection of Jesus. And yet I hadn't, at that point, spent any time talking about his death! That probably felt odd to you, but I hope the reasons for it will now become clear.

Because, you see, one of the worst aspects for the disciples of the humiliating death of Jesus was that it seemed totally disjunct from his life. They had seen him healing all sorts of diseases, as well as taking on (and besting) the religious authorities who'd tried to entrap him. They had seen him show a unique authority, even over the forces of nature. And they had lived with him intimately for three years and seen his teaching and his life to be of a piece with that same unique authority. So they were quite sure this was the Messiah, the Promised One, the Deliverer of the beloved nation.

And then in one night it all collapses, and by the next

night he is dead and buried and everything they had lived for over three years seems a mockery. The authority of his life seems to have no relation to the humiliation and terrible reality of his death.

And then came Easter morning, that first day of the week which every Sunday reminds us of, and the mystery and power of Jesus being raised to life suddenly bursts upon them. Equally suddenly, what had seemed the triumph of plotting and evil was now overturned. If *death* was defeated, then so was the failure, the shame, that went with it. Now it was not only his life that showed a unique authority, but, even more mysteriously, his death also. And so they began to move towards a new and deeper understanding of what Jesus' coming had meant, not simply for themselves, longing but wobbly disciples; not simply for their nation Israel, God's loved and unloving people; not even only for the whole world of their day; but for all people everywhere for all time to come. They began to understand and to preach, and what they preached has meaning, sharp and wonderful meaning, for the Millennium my generation is just concluding, and also for the one your generation and your descendants will live through.

The 'kingdom' and the Cross

In their teaching and preaching these disciples of the earliest Church linked up accounts of Jesus' life and teaching with his death and his words about that death – both before it, for instance at their last supper together, and after it, when he appeared to them and spoke of it. His actions and his teaching in his life on earth had been about 'the kingdom': what it meant that God was sovereign over the earth and how that sovereignty could be known. He showed them that to acknowledge God as sovereign meant not a spiritual abstraction, but an inner turning to God (*metanoia*) with material and social consequences: freedom for the over-burdened – in every sense. Healing for the wounded – in every sense. It meant that the oppressed, those with no 'clout', poor in privilege or influence or goods, would be vindicated. And, most profoundly of all, God's sovereignty gave validity to the hope for life eternal, quenching for ever the sorrowful 'goodbye' of death.

So after his resurrection Christ's followers came to see that his death was also about God's sovereignty, and also about that sovereignty's consequences, both inward and material, for the Covenant people and for the whole world. So their preaching was of the Jesus who 'went about doing good', of how he had suffered death at enemy hands, of how that death had been overcome and what it meant for humankind. At his ascension Jesus had given them the mandate to tell that story to the whole world.

And it is in that perspective of his death that I write to you now from my generation, having received it myself from those who have gone before, having lived by its power through these testing decades, and having found it true.

Why did the world need Jesus?

This is a modern question, isn't it? We ask such questions when we are deeply unsure about issues. And so people ask in my day – and possibly yours – 'Why was the death of Jesus necessary? How can the death of a man 2,000 years ago affect me today?' The earliest Church, however, reflecting on the life and death of Jesus as they now saw them in the light of the Resurrection, identified the state of the human heart, and the consequent condition of human society, as desperately in need of God's intervention. They saw, as millions of Christians have since seen, that rather than the death of Jesus being an accident, it was God's bold and thrilling way of bringing us home to him. We can put what they discerned into current terms: as indeed our own Doctrine Commission did quite recently in its report on salvation. It pointed to three aspects of our human state which shape our need of Jesus.

First, there is *the way we fail God*, falling short in the love and obedience our hearts and lives owe him. It is a failure often pressed deep down under our consciousness, so that though we know we fail him, we often don't acknowledge it. And then again, over against that, is *our fear that God fails us*; that the innocent suffer, and horrible catastrophes happen and God does not overrule them. And then, beyond both those, there is *our sense that death inexorably awaits us*, threatening to make meaningless every noble endeavour or achievement, a fate opaque and inscrutable.

I want to probe these three aspects further, for they will be as true of your times as they are of ours, and were of the world to which Jesus came. Each of them is an aspect of that 'lacking God' which is the human state Jesus came to confront, making for us a way back to God if we are willing to take it.

There's a lot of it about . . .

As A. A. Milne once mysteriously said, 'We are all sinners – at least, the best of us are.' He meant that awareness of being moral and spiritual beings, and of moral and spiritual failure, is the highest awareness of humankind, and the most profoundly true. For, as that same Doctrinal Report put it, there is in us 'a deep-rooted tendency to selfishness which taints all and implicates us all in the web of human evil'. This way of being is what the Bible calls 'sin'. Sin draws us to turn our backs on God in order to seek our own will and desire. And it is the habit of spirit of all of us. It is not simply an aggregation of actions, but an attitude of the heart. It is not even necessarily a series of crimes, for these are civil actions which may or may not be sinful depending on the unjustness of the State and its laws. I think, for example, of the resolute civil defiance of that remarkable woman in Burma, Aung San Suu Kyi, who for nearly twenty years now has courageously opposed the totalitarian regime of her country; resolved, please God, by your day. Or, looking back to the earlier part of my century, the conscientious 'criminals' of Nazi Germany who refused to obey the monstrous orders of a dictator. I fear you will all too certainly have cause for similar examples in your own times.

Let me share an experience which still shocks me. Just a few years ago I stood in a Roman Catholic church in Rwanda with the remains of 5,000 bodies around me – mainly women and children. They had been slaughtered by the Rwandan army; victims of a deliberate genocide which wiped out some 800,000 people. This event had occurred just ten months before my visit, and the victorious invading force, which had formed the next government, decided to leave the bodies where they were as a terrible witness to the evil that was perpetrated on 6th April 1995. All around me were pathetic and familiar signs of our humanity – tiny shoes, fragments of clothing, a purse, a comb, a doll – and then the terrible reality of man's evil – dozens and dozens of skulls, bones and bones, and yet still more bones. The accusing silence seemed to ring with the cries of those slaughtered so awfully. That woman's body still before the altar, hands and feet chopped off; that tiny child's body still in her little dress; the gruesome body of the priest still with his stole around his neck – such human remains were shocking, ugly and deeply moving reminders of the darkness at the heart of humanity. What we would not dream of doing to animals, so insanely we do to our brothers and sisters, simply because they do not belong to our people, our tribe, our colour. . . .

Little wonder that Sir Isaiah Berlin quotes Immanuel Kant approvingly: 'Out of timber so crooked as that from which man is made nothing entirely straight can be built.' And yet from a different 'wood', the wood of the Cross, comes God's answer to our predicament.

Sin must be distinguished from crime, even though there is a clear overlap. Sin is a word that insistently introduces God into our condition. From a Christian perspective, sin presupposes as *essential* to our human identity a profoundly satisfying relationship with God. We do quite wrong to presume that the Bible's account of sin begins with condemnation and judgement. Quite otherwise: it begins with God as Creator who loves his world, God as one creating for us a relationship of loving companionship with him. So to sin is to be so self-directed that this relationship is fractured or ignored or wholly denied.

The story of the Fall in Genesis is a profound analysis of this condition, telling us not about the *origin* of evil – the Bible is not dualistic, though evil is a real presence in its pages – but telling us instead of its mechanism in the human heart. The relationship of joyful and companionable obedience with God is fractured by greed, by mistrust, by the desire for power off limit. Its sequel is contention, refusal of accountability, mutual blame, lust, appalled self-consciousness, and finally a shrinking from the very God whose presence was home to us. The alienation is seen as both individual and corporate. So each of us experiences a separate shrinking away from God in the loneliness and selfishness of individual perversity. Corporately too we are at odds with him, whether we are the Covenant people of Israel or different groupings and societies down the ages.

Jesus identified this as a matter of the heart from which wrong actions came, rather than simply a matter of what we do. He took the concreteness of the Mosaic Law – the Ten Commandments – and showed the profundity of relationship which lay beneath. 'You have heard that it was said to the people long ago, "Do not murder . . ." But I tell you that anyone who is angry with his brother will be subject to judgment. . . . You have heard that it was said, "Do not commit adultery." But I tell you that anyone who looks at a woman lustfully has already committed adultery with her in his heart' (Matthew 5:21–28). St Paul, meditating on the meaning of the Incarnation and the Cross in relation to human nature, focused on the tyranny that this trajectory of the heart exercises over humanity; a tyranny from which only the direct intervention of God could save us. Well did Thomas Fuller somewhat quaintly remark on the way our very pattern of life seems determined by an instinct to vice: 'Pride calls me to the window; gluttony to the table; wantonness to the bed; laziness to the chimney; ambition commands me to go upstairs, and covetousness to come down.'

Thus, Paul suggests, sin has us 'in its grip'; we are 'under sin' in the way a child is 'under' the domination of its parents; sin 'lords it over us' like an emperor leading his booty home in triumph. Such a state is 'killing', it creates despair, and it makes us unable to live in harmony with God, each other and Creation.

Guilty, m'lord

We have made great strides, in this century, in understanding the operation of neurotic and psychopathic feelings. But our great danger has been one I hope your own generation will have moved to correct: the confusion of such illness with that proper sense of guilt which is the appropriate price we pay for being accountable individuals, responsible to God and each other for the moral and spiritual decisions we make. This capacity to choose, spiritually and morally, is our highest dignity. We do ourselves no service by sweeping away the right feeling of guilt that comes when we look squarely at what we do and are. History shows us clearly enough the price we pay for denying guilt. So does our literature. From Shakespeare's *Macbeth*, through great Victorian novelists like George Eliot, to our twentieth-century writers who have so sensitively mapped the darkness of the human spirit – Kafka, Camus, Bellow, Golding, Updike . . . If we try to brush away what they show us of ourselves and our century it will be as though we tried to write off evil itself. For instance, there's a marvellously powerful account of the reality of this *right experience* of guilt in William Golding's very great novel, *Darkness Visible*. (Is he still required reading in your schools, I wonder? I certainly hope so!) In the book we meet a decent, ordinary man, Simon Goodchild, who is a bookseller. And we are given a glimpse of the burden of guilt under which this quite average and good-intentioned man is labouring privately as he remembers a slightly malicious trick he has played on a colleague:

The pressure [of] the memory of his own short-comings . . . intolerable . . . And you could not embark on the long voyage of reparation that could make all well . . . could not do it because, to change the metaphor, this latest piece of wantonness was only a bit on the top of the pile. The pile was a vast heap of rubbish, of ordure, of filthy rags, was a mountain – it did not matter what one did, the pile was too big. Why pick the last bit of filth off the top?

Guilt is the price we pay as moral and spiritual beings for this capacity to know good and evil, and make the choice. As Edward Stein remarked: 'Guilt is the peg on which the meaning of "man" hangs. It is also the peg on which man too often hangs himself.'

'The peg on which man too often hangs himself.' Yes, indeed. The need is precisely this – the impossibility of dealing with guilt. Because, acknowledged, it cannot be assuaged – 'the pile is too big' – and so its effect is destructive; and yet, unacknowledged, it eats at your very soul. It was precisely because of the impossibility and yet the desperate necessity of our dealing with our guilt that God intervened in Jesus. How we may understand the effectiveness of that intervention I'll come to in a minute.

The God who fails?

But your world will know, as mine does, that our guilty fear of God is often matched by anger. Anger that seems justified because of the pointless and unnecessary suffering he seems to allow all around us. The point is well made in Albert Camus' book *The Plague*, where a caring doctor and a caring priest in a village ravaged by plague try to understand what is going on. A child dies agonisingly, and the priest observes that the child's death is revolting to us only because we do not understand it. He suggests, 'Perhaps we should love what we can't understand.' The doctor rejects with anger that pious accommodation. 'No, Father. I have a different idea of love. Until my dying day I shall refuse to love a scheme of things in which children are put to torture.' One is reminded of Bishop David Jenkins' fierce insistence: 'A God who tolerates Auschwitz is the very Devil!'

And that, of course, is the point. God doesn't 'tolerate' it. That, precisely, is what the Cross is all about: God's intolerance not just of evil but of his world's disease and suffering and distresses. The death of Jesus is his unique, long-looked-for-yet-so-unexpected intervention, authoritative and personal. In a moment I want to explore what this means and why it is true, and not only true but effective, and not only effective but for all time. But just at this point I simply want to affirm in the name of all that I have myself lived through and found God at its centre, that he is not a God distanced from our afflictions but 'in all our afflictions he is afflicted'. We do not, that is, live life under a God who is removed from our sufferings, but we believe rather in one who took them to himself and thus destroyed their capacity to destroy.

And the last enemy he destroyed was death. I spoke in my last Letter of what the Resurrection meant in terms of our own being in thrall to mortality. Here I simply want to touch on something that is the corollary of our sense of guilt: the fact that death is associated in the Bible with judgement. When Paul says, 'The sting of death is sin,' he is facing the fact that any question of eternal life has bound up in it issues of facing the God with whom that life is to be spent, since to dwell in his presence is actually one way of defining eternal life. So the Cross confronts our sense of sin, our guilt, and how it encompasses all our questions about innocent suffering. These issues also bear on our fear of the opaqueness and apparent meaninglessness of our inevitable 'end' in death.

Two stories about sin

Jesus told us some of the deepest truths, about our own state and God's response, through stories. Two such stories, as we shall see shortly, are key to our understanding of what the Cross of Jesus means to the world. They are the dark and light of the same truth, and they help us to hold together what, humanly speaking, we find very difficult: the two realities of *justice* and *mercy*.

Perhaps your society will manage it better. My own, currently, is caught up in a 'culture of blame'. Whenever there is a disaster, small or large, the hunt is on for a scapegoat. I actually heard a broadcaster recently interviewing someone who had been caught up in a minor catastrophe, saying, 'Now, who or what can you *blame* for this?' A consequence is an increasing litigiousness, where everyone seeks to take to the law a claim against someone else for their sufferings: from members of the emergency services seeking redress for undue stress to which their job makes them liable, to people claiming against pressurising salesmen who have seduced them into spending more than they ought. (Blame, of course, is as old as chapter 1 of the book of Genesis . . . 'The serpent beguiled me, and I did eat'!)

Such a culture of *blame* is quite different from a culture of *accountability* – though the two are often confused. In the culture of blame we acknowledge the reality of guilt, and of justice, but do not apply them to ourselves. It is always 'the other' who is primarily at fault. In a culture of accountability, by contrast, we ourselves take responsibility for what we do and where we go and what we are.

Now, given all I have said earlier about our knowledge of sin and our sense of guilt in our alienation from God, the Christian faith looks like a classic context for a culture of blame, with God doing the blaming and the rest of us up before the Law (his Law) because of it. But the glorious thing about what Jesus means is, first, that he rejects the culture of blame – as we shall see. And second, that he takes on the culture of accountability, and makes himself the accountable one on our behalf. But, third, most glorious of all, he transforms that culture of accountability, fair but stern as it is, into a quite other culture: a culture of praise. Let his two stories show you what I mean.

The first story is known as 'the parable of the wicked tenants (or husbandmen)' and it is one of the only four of Jesus' stories to appear in all three of the Synoptic Gospels. Moreover, it appears virtually identically in all three versions, which suggests it made a very profound impact on his hearers. It is the tale of a man who established a vineyard. He dug the ground and he set a protective hedge and he planted the vines and he dug a pit for the wine-press – in other words he invested much labour and care to set it up and make it viable. Then he let it out to tenants. The rent was a proportion of the fruit each year to go to him. But when he sent his servant to claim his due in fruit, the tenants beat him up and sent him off empty-handed. And this was repeated several times. So in a last bid to bring the tenants to their senses he sends the 'one other' he has, 'a beloved son', for surely the tenants will respect *him*. Instead, they see in him the last obstacle to taking over the vineyard for themselves. So they throw him out of the vineyard and kill him.

The punch line is inevitable – so much so that in

Matthew's version Jesus gets his listeners to supply it themselves. What will the owner do? They said to him, 'He will bring those wretches to a wretched end . . . and he will rent the vineyard to other tenants, who will give him his share of the crop at harvest time' (Matthew 21:41).

The spiritual meaning of the parable is clear. In terms of justice God's tenants have not only not met their dues, but have actively and destructively rebelled against those dues. Therefore the just and proper and to-be-expected response of God would be to punish and eject those tenants and supplant them. There is nothing effective in the son's death, note. His coming was but the last chance for the tenants. His death squanders it. So the story is a very stark statement of the culture of blame or even of accountability. The tenants are responsible, they have failed, and they must pay the penalty.

We are meant to see here what justice requires. And we do. What is positive in the story is that wrongdoers get their come-uppance; and there is within us a strong sense that this is how life should be. Justice matters.

But when it applies to *us*? When we realise that we as tenants of God have not paid the dues of fruitful love and obedience? We may not have plotted to kill him, but often, often, as individuals and as a nation, we have told him to go away . . . Justice begins to look dark to us.

And so we turn to the second story, known as 'the parable of the prodigal son' – though it equally is called 'the parable of the loving Father and the unforgiving brother'. It's so familiar I won't rehearse it here. You can read it in Luke 15 (verses 11–32). At its heart is the same issue: that of justice. But this time it is set alongside the dynamic of mercy. The parable of the prodigal son sets out for us two conflicting responses to a situation of wrong-doing. One is blame. The other is forgiveness. Some people find this parable difficult because they sympathise with the elder brother; some find it moving because they are comforted by the attitude of the father. How does it balance that first parable? There is of course repentance in it, as there was not in the first. But since the father goes out to meet the returning wrongdoer, forgiveness is offered before the words of penitence are spoken. The key, of course, is in the words of the father: 'He is alive again! . . . was lost, and is found!' And they began to make merry.

The life and death of Jesus form a *living parable* which bridges those two parables and the conflicting attitudes within them. For the just claims of God the Lord of the vineyard are met in Jesus as 'tenant' on our behalf. The 'blame' attitude of the elder brother is rejected because it is life-denying. In its place is the readiness of the father to go out to the wrongdoer, brought home by 'coming to himself'. And the final note of the story is celebration: praise.

Justice and mercy

Those two stories set out creatively for us the human situation which needed Jesus. For if God was to intervene effectively, then both justice and mercy had to be equally served. That is, our failure to obey and love God had to be recognised and somehow so sorted out that the right relationship was re-established, and our debts of 'fruit in due season' discharged. But equally, suffering and bewildered humanity needed to know the reality of the sovereign God among us even in the teeth of horror and distress, loss and dereliction. We need to know he shared it, and yet robbed it of its power to destroy us humanly. So therefore whatever happened on the Cross had to be of power both materially and spiritually. It had to have implications on God's side of things and on the human side of things. It had to serve justice and mercy equally. It had to be something that affected us inwardly, subjectively, but was actual, 'out there', existing even if we didn't acknowledge it. It had to be effective then, and now, and for all time and for the end time.

Now in what senses did the death of Jesus, continuing the work of his life, do any or all of these?

The young hero . . . stripped himself for battle

If we look at the earliest recorded preaching about Jesus, the earliest creed, the earliest hymn, and the earliest theological interpretation of his death, certain convictions come out quite clearly. The preaching emphasises that the whole history of Jesus was within the sovereign design of God (cf. Acts 2:22ff.). The Cross was not an afterthought to Christian proclamation, somehow to be fitted in, but central to it, because it was seen as a part of God's larger plan for finding us and bringing us home. The earliest creed (cf. 1 Corinthians 15, a *paradosis* or 'tradition') insists that 'Christ died for our sins according to the Scriptures'. So 'our sins' and what happened on the Cross are seen from the beginning as linked together by divine intention, and *fruitfully*. (Notice they are 'our' sins, not just those of his enemies or the Jews.)

The remarkable hymn recorded by St Paul in Philippians 2 presents the Cross as part of a life given over in sacrifice. Let me put it in diagrammatic form for you because it reveals the struggle for salvation starting in heaven, descending to the depths of the Cross and then ascending up to glory again. (The numbers refer to the verses.)

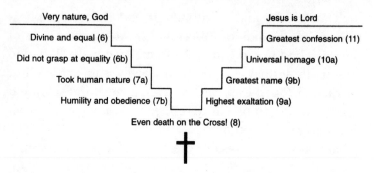

The deliberate steps down to degradation on the Cross show God's wonderful commitment to humanity. The scale of the sacrifice is made clearer by the insistence on the divinity of Christ. *This is very God himself sharing our flesh.* Yet the steps arising to glory represent humanity being taken up into the very life of God.

Now, as I have already said, we shall be very disappointed if we approach the New Testament looking for carefully honed and developed theories of the death of Jesus. They are not there. But what we do find are marvellous glimpses of pictures, images, stories and theological ideas that bring home to us vividly an impression of what it cost God in the suffering of his dear Son. Let me remind you of some of these images and ideas which I am quite confident will be as relevant to your time as they are to mine. Try to think of the various interpretations I'm about to describe to you as a series of perspectives on so huge an event that all we can do is gaze at it from ever new angles, consider it from different ways of seeing, ponder it and take each understanding into our hearts to feed us.

'To feed us' . . . those words instantly remind us of the Last Supper and Jesus' own words there before his death. That meal was, in the context of Jesus' nationality and

formal practice of the Jewish faith, a sacrificial one. It was the Passover meal, that annual celebration of God delivering his people from their life of slavery in Egypt. So Jesus asks his followers to think of the bread and the wine of that meal as symbolic in a new way of God's deliverance from slavery, because they epitomise the body and the blood he is to give. 'Take and eat,' he says, 'in remembrance of me. This is my body . . . this is my blood.'

So 'Jesus as sacrifice' is one of the ways in which we can think about what the Cross of Jesus means. Part of our right relationship with God is worship. We do not now have the background of cultic sacrificial worship which made this way of thinking so immediate and helpful to those seeking to understand in the days of the early Church. But we do still have the sense that God is to be worshipped with a pure heart. And that is an offering we are unable to bring him of ourselves, unaided. But through Jesus we can. For the disciples and their immediate successors, the whole culture of cultic sacrifices made on the Day of Atonement, such as is explored in relation to Christ's sacrificial offering in the Epistle to the Hebrews, meant that in Jesus a sacrifice had been made which achieved reconciliation with God in a way which animal sacrifices could not. Sacrifice, of course, is still a very meaningful way of understanding the Cross. Even though we all find it difficult to understand how the sacrifice of a good person nearly 2,000 years ago 'paid' for our salvation, we all know the remarkable power of the way parents will sacrifice everything for their children, and the splendid, devoted, self-giving of those who care for the marginalised, the unloved and dying. Sacrifice is an important 'way in' to interpreting the Cross.

Another glorious image of the Cross is *reconciliation*. When we have done something to spoil a relationship, we look for some adequate way of saying sorry. Words aren't always enough, or don't feel enough. Because something has changed in our relationship, we seek means to move it on, to change it yet again – not back because there is no going back, but forward into an even deeper relationship. The steps we take, whether they are offerings of flowers or attempts to give pleasure in some other concrete way, take account of the fact that reconciliation has a material, a concrete dimension. It isn't just talk. 'It's too easy to say sorry and think that's put it right,' my father used to say when I had been naughty. 'Sorry how much?' I used to think.

And so there is what someone has recently called 'the endless search for the reparation deed'. How may we find anything adequate when the breakdown is between God and us? We can't. So God makes amends on both sides, so to speak. In Jesus all humanity was caught up in an expression of sorrow and suffering and obedience. But in Jesus also, God himself was paying the agonising price of restoring the relationship and getting things right. It wasn't in any sense a legal exchange, though some have interpreted it legalistically and it certainly stands up to the scrutiny of the most rigorous law. Nor was it simply giving us a perfect example to follow – which is another way of looking at the Cross (one pressed by Abelard long ago). No, it was deeper than that. It was recognising that putting relationships right is always costly, and since humanity couldn't match the price of itself, God did. So we get what is known as the 'Latin' theory of atonement, associated with great theologians like St Anselm, where God intervenes for us in our desperate situation of alienation and fear, because we can't do it for ourselves. (Indeed, as the film producer Woody Allen once memorably put it in the mouth of one of his characters, 'For all

my education, accomplishments and so-called wisdom
. . . I can't fathom my own heart.' So much good theology
comes inadvertently from films and books!)

But pause to consider. Normally, when peace negotia-
tions are being conducted, the injured party expects the
other to fund the reparations. Yet God's reconciliation
took the form of God giving his best for us. The cost is
borne by him alone: there is no division between the Lord
Jesus and God the Father. They are wholly at one in the
work of reconciliation. And it is for us. For us. We can
never overstate the overwhelming generosity of God's
love: 'For God was pleased to have all his fullness dwell
in him, and through him to reconcile to himself all things
. . . by making peace through his blood, shed on the cross'
(Colossians 1:20). St Anselm, my predecessor, suggested
that our only possible response to such lovingkindness
must be that of submission: 'O Lord, draw my whole self
into your love . . . let your love seize my whole being; let
it possess me completely.' That is reconciliation: not God
being reconciled to us – he is always the instigator of the
amends – but sad, battered, wandering humanity 'come
to itself' through the love of Jesus, coming home at last,
reconciled.

My own name reminds me of another great Biblical
image, namely *redemption*. I am sad to say that very few
people use this word 'redemption' in ordinary parlance.
It is a pity because it is such a beautiful word which is so
common to human experience. It means 'buying back'
and is so familiar to us all. So to my name – 'Carey'. Carey
Street in London used to be lined with pawn-brokers'
shops. 'Going up Carey Street' was Victorian slang for
being broke. If you were hard-up you could take a ring,
heirloom or whatever and hand it over. In return you
would be given a sum of money to help you over your

crisis. You would never own that valuable possession again, though, unless you could save up enough to 'redeem' it with not only the original sum but a steep interest. The basic concept of redemption is available to us, therefore, from our own social history.

The sense in which the New Testament used it to describe what Jesus did for us becomes even clearer when we take an example from its own era. An inscription was found in Greece at the beginning of this century, dating from New Testament times. It read, 'Sosibus sold to the Pythian Apollo a female slave named Nicaea at the price of three minae of silver for freedom.' The names of three witnesses are added.

We can work out what the inscription meant. Nicaea, a slave, had over several years saved up three minae of silver: that was her price. She had paid it into the temple, and was now bought by her god. That god had paid the ransom to the one who owned her. It was a standard formula for obtaining freedom. Now she was free, albeit 'religiously' the slave of Apollo. How symbolic it is that slavery to the god should set her free! She had been 'redeemed'. In Mark 10:45 it says that the Son of Man came 'to give his life as a ransom for many'.

In my imagination I can see Nicaea walking from that temple a free person, dizzy, exhilarated by the sense of freedom, no longer a slave to someone else! Free, free, free . . . The New Testament throbs with that kind of experience. However, the New Testament gives it a particular and special twist. We are free, but not free to do what we like. St Paul puts it like this: 'You were bought with a price. Therefore honour God with your bodies.' Christian freedom, you see, is not freedom to do anything we like but freedom we offer back to the Redeemer 'whose service is perfect freedom'.

Another way of looking at what the Cross means is by reminding ourselves of that language of Paul, about sin being a tyrant over us. Clearly, if we are at the mercy of a tyrant, we need a *champion*, someone who will fight for us and set us free. So one picture way of understanding what Jesus did on the Cross is that of a champion or soldier who takes over our battle and defeats the dictator, finally leading him out chained and captive. The value of this way of looking at what Jesus means is that it takes seriously the sheer reality and power of evil. It also gets us away from the sterile argument about to whom Jesus paid the redemption fee: to the Devil? Surely not! It would be immoral! To God, then? Surely not! The God who gave his best for us is not a God who is, in character, one to hold us to ransom. The argument shows why these must all be treated as snapshots or glimpses of what was happening on the Cross. They can't be put to definitive analysis.

But Jesus as both our representative and champion: yes, that matches the overwhelming sense of release that we can all know because of him, and which Paul describes: 'For what I do is not the good I want to do; no, the evil I do not want to do – this I keep doing . . . What a wretched man I am! Who will rescue me from this body of death? Thanks be to God – through Jesus Christ our Lord!' (Romans 7:18, 24–25).

Jesus as *Victor* in the fight against evil on our behalf – that is one of the most enduring interpretations through the Christian centuries, even though the trappings of the picture change. I wonder if in your English classes you occasionally study the writings of the Anglo-Saxon period; what we call, disparagingly, the early Dark Ages. From that period comes a remarkable poem called 'The Dream of the Rood'. The unknown Anglo-Saxon poet who meditated on Christ as a young warrior mounting the Cross to do battle, was seized of the same truth as those who in this my own century have invoked the saving power of Christ's Passion as they have confronted the vilest evil in death camps and amid 'ethnic-cleansing' horrors:

The 'Rood' – Tree of Crucifixion – is speaking:

> Then the young Hero – it was God Almighty –
> Strong and steadfast, stripped himself for battle;
> He climbed up on the high gallows, constant in his
>   purpose,
> Mounted it in sight of many, mankind to ransom.
> Horror seized me when the Hero clasped me,
> But I dared not bow or bend down to earth,
> Nor falter, nor fall; firm I needs must stand.
> I raised up a Rood, a royal King I bore,
> The High King of Heaven: hold firm I must.
> They drove dark nails through me, the dire wounds still
>   show,
> Cruel gaping gashes, yet I dared not give as good.
> They taunted the two of us; I was wet with teeming
>   blood,
> Streaming from the warrior's side when he sent forth
>   his spirit . . .

The poet ends in prayer:

> May the Lord be my friend,
> Who erstwhile on earth endured bitter throes,
> Suffered on the gallows-tree for the sins of men.
> He loosed us from bondage and life he gave to us
> And a home in Heaven . . .
> Christ the Son of God journeyed as a Conqueror,
> Mighty and Victorious, when with many in his train,
> A great company of souls, he came to God's Kingdom.

I hope that you find it as wonderful and as moving a poem as I do. I love its strong language and beautiful images which bring home the physical suffering that the Lord endured. Yes, the *God who suffers.*

This picture of victory through Christ enduring heroic suffering, though its trappings are those of heroic combat as in Anglo-Saxon times, yet leads us into a way of thinking about what the Cross means to us which is very much of this last half-century. You in your generation may have taken it much further. For in these last decades we have become aware as perhaps never before of the scale and depth and universality and intractability of human suffering, through its immediacy to us all by radio and TV screen. And so the long-held belief that God himself was impassible, i.e. not vulnerable to suffering, has begun to dissolve. Many theologians are now exploring what it means for us if we do not think of Christ as simply suffering in his human nature, but as wholly suffering. That is, God was in him, suffering with us. This is how the theologians of *The Mystery of Salvation* put it:

> The only ultimately satisfactory response to the problem of unmerited or disproportionate [human] suffering is to believe that our creator, through a wonderful act – at once of self-limitation and of self-expression, is present in the darkest affliction, shares our pain, bears our sorrows, and sustains us through it all, creating good in spite of evil, so revealing the true nature of divine power as showing mercy and pity.

One of our hymns by W. H. Vanstone puts it powerfully in this way:

> Thou art God: no monarch Thou
> Thron'd in easy state to reign;
> Thou art God, Whose arms of love
> Aching, spent, the world sustain.

Let me now pass to my final image which, although taken from the law courts of the first century, is as relevant to my day as I suspect it is to yours. Let me put it in this hypothetical way. One day, a tradesman agrees with me to do a particular job at a particular price, but the contract is broken by him with considerable inconvenience to myself. The situation demands justice, redress; and it also involves a breakdown of trust. The contractual relationship is at an end.

St Paul in particular saw such a concept of justice as a helpful way of understanding what God has done for us in Christ. Even though we are guilty and unjust, Christ's righteousness compensates for us.

Of course, there is a huge problem here related to the human way of perceiving what is right and wrong. For example, if God simply forgives us when we sin and declares us 'just', isn't that a denial of reality? The joke about second-hand car dealers contains a serious truth: if you are let down by a second-hand car dealer, trust in members of this fraternity is the first casualty. So how can God – the basis and origin of all justice – go on 'employing' us as his own people even when we break our contract with him? Isn't that a denial of the truth of things?

These questions lie behind the picture of what Jesus means as *the one who justifies*. It would be easy to become very complex here. Instead, I want to say just two things about it. The first comes from the insight with which Martin Luther was seized, which became part of our Reformed – and then, thank God, our wider – Christian heritage. It was simply this: we need to keep fast hold of the truth that we can't *earn* our way into heaven, because we are not capable of keeping to the contract. So, instead, we get there by God's generosity – 'grace' is the word.

And that grace, generosity, is expressed through the love and self-expenditure Jesus shows in his dying. All we have to do – but it's a big step – is to trust that generosity, and not start making excuses or trying to keep the contract by ourselves. The famous Pauline phrase which sums all this up is that we have been justified or saved 'by grace through faith' (Romans 3:24; Ephesians 2:8).

The second thing I want to say follows from this. For effectively what God did in Jesus was to give us a new contract. That is, not only did he not demand redress. Not only did he not write us off. Instead, he gave us a new and better contract ('covenant' is the word used) and underwrote it himself. That is, Jesus became the one with whom and through whom the new contract was written, with the commitment that all the resources were already up front and there would never be any question of their running out. Theologians have sometimes used the term 'substitution' of the breathtaking transaction that the Bible so daringly speaks about. St Paul speaks of Christ becoming an 'accursed thing' for us on the gibbet. Jesus takes upon himself the *fullness* of humanity. Think about it for one moment; think of the mountain of filth and wantonness which that meant burdening himself with as we saw earlier in Simon Goodchild's misery. And what none of us could do, God did, in removing not just the last few deposits of mess, but the whole of it. A cosmic cleansing. And so we are enabled, prodigal sons and daughters, to 'come to ourselves' and come home to the Father. We were lost and are found; were dead and are alive again. And the whole of it is love. Because that was the measure of love which was showed by God the Father and God the Son in what happened on the Cross. And love is the currency of that contract, as it is of all God's dealings with his Creation.

The love that moves the sun and other stars . . .

Love is the currency of the contract. If I communicate nothing else to you of those things which have sustained us through this dark century, the things Jesus means to us, this above all I would press. The story of the love on the Cross began with Creation. It was continued in God's dealings with his errant people, as they showed themselves unable to live peaceably and fruitfully with each other, the natural world, and God himself. It began to take on a very precisely focused history in God's calling out of the nation of Israel to be a blessing to the world. And the life on Earth, and death, of Jesus, was the climax of that history of blessing through a people called to be his love in the world. For in his life of serving and his death of love, God in Jesus plumbed the depths of our estrangement and showed us how to come home. That, in the end, is what the Cross means: a bridge across the chasm, a road home for us.

So we need to make the decision to cross the bridge, if we haven't already. Cross the bridge and take the road home to God. For we shan't ever really begin to understand what the Cross means for us and our times until we risk trusting it, surrendering ourselves to what it tells us of God, and living accordingly. When that happens, you will find, as my generation has found and all those crowding generations of wondering Christians of the past, that existence begins to make sense perhaps for the first time – though not the kind of sense the world much cares for. You'll find yourself thinking, 'At last I begin to understand the wonder of God's love and the joy of living for him . . .'

I'm sorry that this has been such a long Letter. I felt it necessary to dwell on all the implications of the Cross because the death of Jesus alone can make sense of *our* dying; death, so terrible and so personal. But never final, because the Cross is our passport to the kingdom. And how God sustains us in that journey – through the gift of the Spirit – well, that will be the burden of my next Letter.

In the meantime, my dear friends of the next century, may our Lord inspire your lives with the assurance that you are fully accepted in him.

Yours in great thankfulness,

George

LETTER 9

The Holy Spirit and 'the Cloud with the Three Faces'

Dear Friends of the Future,

Some years ago I had a profound experience of the Holy Spirit which I have recounted in another book. There was nothing particularly ecstatic or dramatic about it; it happened to me at the point of questioning about the Christian faith and at the point of deep dissatisfaction with my own spiritual journey. The point about my quiet and simple rediscovery of the Spirit was a new awareness of the Holy Trinity.

I remembered again that encounter with the holy God when I paid a recent visit to a village church in the diocese of Salisbury. It was a very unusual church in that although it was in a rather traditional village, the congregation had quadrupled in recent years because of a charismatic vicar and the impact of preaching and teaching which focused on the Holy Spirit. I was very moved by the testimony of an eighty-seven-year-old lady who described her own pilgrimage of faith. 'I used to be a special Sunday Christian,' she said. 'But thanks to this church I found the real meaning of God through a new experience of the Holy Spirit. Now every Sunday is special.'

Now, let me begin this Letter by saying that there are not two sorts of Christians – those who have had charismatic experiences and those who have not had them. Indeed not. In a fundamental sense *all* Christians are 'charismatics' (gifted with the Holy Spirit) and that understanding is the important presupposition of this Letter.

So the only way I can talk with you at this point – as I must – about the Holy Spirit and what we learn from him about the nature of God himself, is through the experience you and I have in common, of the grace of the God and Father of our Lord Jesus Christ. For the *experience* of that grace – not so much its source as its actualising in our hearts – that is the work of the Holy Spirit.

But the problem for so many Christians is that somehow the 'mystery of the Trinity has lost its moorings in common Christian experience', to quote Edmund Hill, a Roman Catholic writer. Or, as the Doctrine Commission of the Church of England put it fairly recently in its Report: 'Although the Christian faith is distinctive in its "Trinitarian structure", there is little "popular" engagement with the doctrine.' It is strange that this should be so, as Sunday after Sunday we recite a Trinitarian faith in the Eucharist in the words of the Nicene Creed. The Report goes on: 'Here God is seen as eternally triune, which means that in the Godhead there are united three "persons" ("hypostases") who are distinguishable only by number and relation to one another, and inseparable in their activity.' This doesn't, as the Commission confesses, exactly grab the Western imagination. Perhaps the majority of practising Christians have considerable sympathy with the Japanese gentleman who is reported to have said to a Christian in that delightful and picturesque way so typical of the Japanese: 'The Holy Father I understand, the Holy Son I understand – but the Holy Bird I do not understand at all.'

And yet, my dear fellow Christians of the future, it is the wonder of the work of the Holy Spirit – yes, the Holy Bird – the mystery of his 'agency', his enabling, which makes it possible for me to be communicating now with you about the things of God. For, as I hope we shall see in the course of this Letter, though some have urged that what we call the Holy Spirit is simply another name for God-in-action, yet it becomes increasingly clear that first the disciples, then the young Church, and then the Church through history, and the individual members of it, experienced something which had the quality of a personal presence. Here was another aspect of the God whom the disciples had already learned to know as 'Abba, Father', and had already also learned to know as 'Jesus, the Christ, the Son'. So the sense of the Person of the Spirit began to grow, and with it the gathering understanding of God as 'Three, and yet One': of whom we must neither 'confound the persons nor divide the substance', to use the traditional formula.

Part of our difficulty in talking about the Spirit, and therefore about the Trinity, lies in the vague and confused images or pictures we often have of what we're talking about. When in a moment we start looking more closely at what we may know of the Holy Spirit, we shall find that we have in fact some very concrete pictures available: of a dove, of fire, of a rushing, mighty wind. But Bishop David Jenkins put it both truly and vividly when he commented that for most people their picture of the Trinity, insofar as they had one at all, was vague and speculative, a 'sort of cloud with three faces'.

There are some famous icons of the Eastern Church which suggest a much clearer and more sharply focused idea of the Trinity than that. And, incidentally, they show a way of thinking about the three Persons of God which is in some contrast to our own, Western image. For when we get away from anything as unformulated as the 'cloud with three faces', the most widespread idea here of the Trinity is of God the Father as older, bearded; God the Son as younger, with flowing hair; and God the Spirit as the dove – 'the holy bird' – flying between Father and Son. Great masterpieces of Western art, through centuries, have portrayed the Trinity in this way.

By contrast, Eastern pictures of the Trinity usually portray the three Persons as of the same age. (This, incidentally, immediately gives us a stronger sense of their total equity and mutuality.) Probably the best-known icon is that of the three Persons of the Trinity as the three mysterious beings who visited Abraham to tell of his future son. They are portrayed as three persons of much the same age, sitting in mutual harmony round that table which is to become the symbol of so many things: altar, eucharistic table of feasting, the banqueting of heaven … But there is another Eastern image of the Trinity, equally telling: that of a head with, yes, three faces – all of the same age, each face looking in a different direction, so that we have two profiles and one full face impression of the three Persons of the Godhead. Two of those Persons are familiar to us, as they were to the disciples. But what of the third? Of whom do we speak at the service of Holy Communion when we affirm, in the Creed, 'We believe in the Holy Spirit, the Lord, the giver of life'?

'The Holy Spirit … giver of life'

Others have pointed out that even the Apostles' Creed, which is the simplest form in which we affirm together regularly our Christian faith, fits all its articles into a Trinitarian formula. After the nature and work of Father and Son have been described, we speak of the Spirit and, by implication, of how he is the 'giver of life' to us, as we already experience it or trust to know it, in 'the holy catholic church and the communion of saints'; in the 'resurrection of the body'; and in the 'life everlasting'. What is our basis for this emphasis on the Spirit as the divine agent of life itself, life unquenchable and beyond (though including) the physical?

The gospel story is our best way into this mystery. The gospel story as it looks back to the Creation itself, and forward to the Last Things. (There is continuity and discontinuity between the Old and New Testament accounts of the Spirit, but for the moment I want to focus on what is continuous between them.) For if we follow the grand design of the gospel story, we meet the Spirit in the second verse of the Bible, in that awesome account of Creation where, while the earth was as yet 'without form and void' – a sort of archetypal soup – and all was darkness 'upon the face of the deep', there was 'the Spirit of God', 'moving over the face of the waters'.

The root meaning of the word used here, as elsewhere, for Spirit, is 'breath', 'wind'; and indeed 'wind of God' is offered as an alternative translation. The Spirit of God – that Person within the Godhead here associated with the creation of the world – is also implied, therefore, when in another Creation story God made man of dust from the ground and 'breathed into his nostrils the breath of life, and the man became a living being' (Genesis 2:7).

'Breath', 'wind' and the mystery of the gift of life itself – that which distinguishes the clay model of a man from a living being. The Old Testament develops some of these themes in relation to the Spirit, but I want, for simplicity's sake, to move on to the very concrete way we encounter the Spirit in the story of Jesus. For we are to encounter the Spirit again as 'breath', 'wind'; but this time a mighty and rushing wind which 'filled all the house' at Pentecost. And this is the climax of the story of Jesus, which I shall look at in detail in a moment. Before we reach that climax, however, we have met the Spirit materially earlier in Christ's story. For he is the agent of Christ's conception. Mary is promised, 'The Holy Spirit will come upon you, and the power of the Most High will overshadow you' (Luke 1:35). 'Life', 'creation' and divine 'power' are invested – as is made visible later in Jesus' story, when he is baptised by John in the River Jordan, and 'heaven was opened and the Holy Spirit descended on him in bodily form like a dove. And a voice came from heaven: "You are my Son, whom I love; with you I am well pleased"' [or, as a variant reading puts it, 'Today I have begotten thee'] (Luke 3:21–22).

It is not surprising that so many major painters of Christian subjects have chosen to depict this scene, for it is one of the very rare moments in the Christian story when all three Persons of the Trinity are described as accessible to human physical perception: the Son in his human presence; the Father, heard by some as 'a voice'; and the Spirit 'in bodily form'. Whatever else was involved in this high moment in the story of Jesus, it is clear that he was understood to have received, through the agency of the Holy Spirit, a unique and distinctive 'power' with which to confront the power of evil: 'Jesus, full of the Holy Spirit, returned from the Jordan and was led by the Spirit in the desert, where for forty days he was tempted by the devil' (Luke 4:1–2). All four Gospels agree that the baptism of Jesus was a time when the Spirit came upon him not only as empowerment for ministry, but as a sign to all that he was Son of the most high God. This sign is continued throughout his ministry, in that, by contrast with John the Baptist, Jesus will baptise others with the Holy Spirit and (according to Matthew and Luke) 'with fire'.

'Breath/wind'; 'dove'; 'fire': the concrete pictures of this Person of the Godhead, ways of seeing him. And his characteristic gifts: 'power'; 'life' itself; and also, as we shall see, 'abundance' and 'unity'. What we must keep in mind constantly when meditating on the mystery of the Holy Spirit is that just as we know him in our lives in his opening of our understanding, in his enabling us to pray aright, in his inspiring us to the life of faith and then confirming us in it with power, so that same ceaseless activity of the Spirit was present in the incarnate life of Jesus. For it wasn't as though the Father and the Spirit took a rest while the Son, in the Person of Jesus, got on with this particular part of the divine job. The Father, Son and Spirit are to be thought of as eternally present to each other all the time, eternally interacting with each other in love – a love that flows between and yet beyond them, eternally expending their common and yet their particular resources on the needs of Creation. Hence they are to be thought of as each having his own work – yet being inseparable, they work inseparably: whether in the creation of the universe, in redeeming it, or in the final consummation of history on the Last Day.

So the Holy Spirit is present in Jesus' ministry, sustaining and empowering it. Present, too, most certainly, in those long nights of prayer spent up on the mountain. Sometimes we are given a glimpse which makes this presence of the Spirit in the life and work of the Son absolutely explicit. For instance, as the ministry of Jesus begins we are told (by Luke) of the return to Jesus' synagogue at Nazareth, of his taking the scroll and reading, 'The Spirit of the Lord is on me, because he has anointed me to preach good news to the poor. He has sent me to proclaim freedom for the prisoners and recovery of sight for the blind' (4:18). And then claiming it as a precise description of his own ministry: 'Today this scripture is fulfilled in your hearing.' This means precisely what it says. It is not only a messianic claim (and would be heard as such) since it fulfils the prophecies recorded in the Old Testament of 'the one to come'; more than this, it is reminding us that the divine work of Jesus is not separate at any point from the life of the Father and the Spirit, but always they are involved in it, present in it.

Thus the agonised cry from the Cross, 'My God, my God, why have you forsaken me?', takes on a very special significance. For if the very nature of the Trinity is that the three Persons of it are for ever at one, then the experience 'as of' aloneness ('as of' because it could not be a reality, but 'felt' as a reality) must have been the ultimate in suffering. Suffering such as only the divine could know, since only the divine lives in such unbroken and wholly loving, interacting unity. 'We may not know, we cannot tell, what pains he had to bear; but we believe it was for us he hung and suffered there.' The inescapable logic is that the Spirit and the Father suffered with the Son as the Son suffered the horror of isolation on the Cross.

And if that is the case, then the same is most certainly true of the Resurrection. Indeed, the particular gifts of the Spirit's agency – 'life', 'power' – are clearly involved. We have no picture at all of how that agency of power and life was projected. But the results are clearly testified: a great door-stone rolled away, abandoned grave-clothes and an empty tomb.

The coming of the Spirit at Pentecost

1. *The witness of the Gospel of John*

All this lies behind the account of the gift of the Spirit to the disciples at Pentecost. And to it we must add the special understanding of the Spirit which the Gospel of John offers us, in what Jesus himself said of the Spirit who was to come. There the word Jesus is quoted as using to describe the Spirit is, in the Greek, 'Paraclete'. The verb from which it is derived means, literally, 'called alongside', and so Jesus' word for the Spirit has been variously interpreted as 'Comforter', 'Intercessor', 'Preacher', 'Advocate', 'Helper' and 'Champion'. For myself, I prefer the notion of 'the Champion', because it conveys the vigorous image of one who not only stands alongside us as our companion, but as one who takes our side in mighty defence. In John 14:6 Jesus is described as promising that such a Paraclete will be sent to be with his followers after he is himself no longer with them in the flesh. So the Spirit, the Paraclete, will maintain the strong ministry the disciples experienced through Jesus, in us and with us.

John's Gospel gives us more detail of this 'Champion' whose coming is promised. His ministry is to be with them 'for ever' as a continuation of Jesus' ministry, for he is described by Jesus as 'another' Paraclete (John 14:16). (In other words, Jesus himself has been, in his earthly ministry, a 'Paraclete', a 'Champion'. And if the Son does not 'go away', 'this' Paraclete 'will not come' [John 16:7], but if the Son leaves his followers, then he will 'send him' to them.) And again, we have a glimpse of the inseparability of Father, Son and Spirit, for this 'Champion', the Holy Spirit, is one 'whom the Father will send' in the name of the Son (John 14:26). Moreover, his task is directly and explicitly related to that of Jesus: he will testify on behalf of the Son (John 15:26), and ultimately the Spirit's work will prove to 'bring glory' to the Son 'by taking what is [the Son's] and making it known' to them (John 16:14).

Thus, on the one hand, John's Gospel shows Jesus as strongly emphasising the profound interconnectedness between the promised 'Champion' and himself. On the other hand, he also emphasises that the disciples will themselves be drawn into that same relationship, a continuation of the relationship they have experienced with Jesus, for 'he lives with you and will be in you' (John 14:17). He is in them as the 'Spirit of truth', the sort of truth which stands over against the self-deception of 'the world'; and which the world 'cannot receive' – as though its receptivity is blocked on the wavelength of spiritual reality. In the light of that truth the world will be convicted 'of guilt in regard to sin and righteousness and judgment [error]' (John 16:8).

The promised Spirit, therefore, who did indeed come upon the disciples at Pentecost, is inseparable from the life of the Father and the Son, and is the agent, in the same way that Jesus was the agent, of the work of the Godhead on earth, at the close of the Son's earthly ministry. That work, whether of Father, Son or Spirit, is all one; and therefore the Spirit's continuation of it among us for ever is to lead us into ever deeper understanding of, and commitment to, the love of God the Father, as demonstrated and made effective for us by God the Son. The insistence on the Spirit's nature as 'truth' draws our attention to the holiness and purity of God. (The image of the 'flames' of Pentecost is not least about the purifying nature of this Spirit of truth. Therefore those who make plausible claims of experience of the Spirit which are not reflected in their lifestyle must face the reality of this divine truth and holiness.)

2. *The witness of Luke*

In the Old Testament 'the Spirit' was received only by individuals called out for a special life role, or even a specific one-off task for God. So, for instance, 'the Spirit' indwelt the great prophets of the past, and was perhaps understood as a synonym for God's power. The continuity and discontinuity of Old and New Testaments is marked here. For, although the Judaism of Jesus' time had a place for 'the Spirit', the understanding was still of a dynamic force rather than in terms of 'Person'. But the New Testament gospel story of the coming of Christ and the power of what happened at Cross and tomb describes floodgates of blessing released upon the whole gathering of Christ's followers. For, just as we have seen that the Holy Spirit was a part of the mystery of the Resurrection, now we see that same agency of life – divinely given life – at work in the disciples. In a real sense, this was their resurrection, and with it, life for them in a new condition and dimension, that of the newly born Church.

Scholars have seen in the event of Pentecost interesting parallels between the giving of the Law, in the Old Testament account, which made of Israel a holy people, and the coming of the Spirit, in the New Testament account, which made of Christ's disciples a 'new' Israel, a holy Church. And indeed, the feast of Pentecost in the Jewish calendar had come to be a commemoration of the giving of the divine Law at Mount Sinai, associated therefore with the images of fire and wind. From that first Christian Pentecost onwards, the Spirit was a gift to all followers of Christ, usually received at baptism (Acts 2:42). In the power of that Spirit the first Christians evangelised, taught the faith, built their churches and lived their Christian lives. Indeed, though the fifth book of the New Testament is referred to as the 'Acts of the Apostles', it would be more accurate to speak of the 'Acts of the Holy Spirit'. For the work of the ascended Christ continues through the activity of the Spirit in the Church. The book throbs with his life and power.

How is this powerful new life in the Spirit character-ised? By 'abundance': the house where they are sitting is 'filled' with 'the sound . . . from heaven like the rush of a mighty wind'; the disciples themselves are all 'filled' with the Holy Spirit. By 'purity': the 'tongues of fire' which accompany the mighty wind are 'distributed and rest on each one of them'. (We are very clearly reminded of the vision of the prophet Isaiah [Isaiah 6] when 'the train of [the Lord's] robe *filled* the temple', and the seraphs called to each other adoration of the holiness of the Lord, 'the whole earth . . . *full* of his glory'. And Isaiah is purified for the purpose of telling out the message of God, by a live coal from the altar touched to his lips.) The new life in the Spirit is characterised, too, by 'boldness': they begin to speak, from this point on, with clarity and sureness about Jesus and his lordship. And by 'unity': the fellowship among this group becomes a matter of remark, and that symbol of human division, the barrier of language, is destroyed.

All these characteristics are meditated upon in the letters of St Paul, and so it is to his profound account of the Spirit that I next want to take you. For in these letters we have glimpses of how the Spirit draws God's children into ever deeper understanding of God's loving plan for them, and empowers them in the quality of life which is the only proper consequence of that understanding. That is, **the Holy Spirit shows us what God is like, in Christ Jesus, and then helps us to be like him.** Paul gives us – not systematically but through a series of insights in his letters to different churches – some indication of what this means.

3. *The witness of Paul to the Spirit*

Paul's letters were all written within the period AD 49–64, and in them we can discern the way the apostle and the young Church were working out their theology in the light of their experience. So it is a 'theology in process' we are engaging with here; a process stimulated by their actual experience of the Spirit as Person. So, while Paul's starting point is that God is one, that experience leads him to recognise a distinctiveness not only about Jesus Christ as the Son of God, but about the Spirit. There is a little piece of narrative in Acts which indicates this very clearly. Paul has arrived at Ephesus (Acts 19:1) where he finds some disciples:

> He asked them, 'Did you receive the Holy Spirit when you believed?'
>
> They answered, 'No, we have not even heard that there is a Holy Spirit.'
>
> So Paul asked, 'Then what baptism did you receive?'
>
> 'John's baptism,' they replied.
>
> Paul said, 'John's baptism was a baptism of repentance. He told the people to believe in the one coming after him, that is, in Jesus.' On hearing this, they were baptised into the name of the Lord Jesus. When Paul placed his hands on them, the Holy Spirit came on them, and they spoke in tongues and prophesied. There were about twelve men in all. (Acts 19:2–7)

The distinctiveness of the Spirit, and yet his inseparability from Jesus, Son of God, comes out clearly in this incident. That he is to be understood personally is glimpsed also in relation to these same disciples of Ephesus, for in the letter to the Ephesians reference is made to his capacity to 'grieve' (Ephesians 4:30). Something similar is implied in Paul's first letter to the Corinthians, where (6:19) he speaks of the dwelling of the Holy Spirit in our bodies: 'Do you not know that your body is a temple of the Holy Spirit, who is in you, whom you have received from God? You are not your own; you were bought at a price. Therefore honour God with your body.' (Earlier in the same letter [3:16] Paul had asked them, 'Don't you know that you yourselves are God's temple and that God's Spirit lives in you?') Again, the distinctiveness of the Spirit and yet his inseparability from both Father and Son is implied.

Perhaps the strongest assertion of this is again in the first letter to the Corinthians, where Paul states emphatically that 'no-one can say, "Jesus is Lord," except by the Holy Spirit' (12:3). Similarly, 'God sent the Spirit of his Son into our hearts, the Spirit who calls out "Abba, Father"' (Galatians 4:6). What is constantly before us is the sense of a distinct Person who is nevertheless so inseparably at one with Father and Son that he can be variously described by Paul as 'the Spirit of God' (Romans 8:9), 'the Spirit of him who raised Jesus' (Romans 8:11); and yet also (in the same letter) 'the Spirit of Christ' (Romans 8:9).

The Spirit's nature and work: 'procession' and 'mission'

From all of this it will be clear that when we think about the Spirit, it is far harder to characterise him in relation to the Father and the Son – what is technically known as the 'procession' of the Spirit in the Trinity – than it is to understand him and recognise him through his work, his activity – what is technically known as the 'mission' of the Spirit. We have noted two moments when that mission became visible: at the baptism of Christ, and on the Day of Pentecost. In a moment I want to look more fully with you at how most followers of Christ have best known the Spirit: through his work within and among them, and the fruits which follow. But before we leave for the moment our thinking about the nature of the Spirit, and his inseparability in our thinking from the Father and the Son, we might just notice an awe-inspiring implication: these glimpses which Paul describes, and which the Church through the ages has continued to have, of a Person distinct and yet inseparable from the Father God and God the Son, mean that the perfect mutual love between Father and Son (which we see most powerfully in the ministry of Jesus) is never 'exclusive'. As the Doctrine Commission put it, there is not and cannot be 'mutual self-absorption'. Therefore because of the existence of the Spirit as a separate Person, 'the relation of the Father and the Son is open to a world of possible beings'. All Creation and its future lies in that truth.

The work of the Holy Spirit

1. AS AGENT TO THE WORLD OF THE UNITY WITHIN THE GODHEAD

We have already seen in the gospel story that the Spirit is the Agent of God as he reaches out in love. We saw it in the accounts of Creation, in God's dealings with his holy people, and supremely in the ministry of Jesus. But now the further wonder of the ministry of the Spirit begins to unfold (remember that in him we have the direct continuation of the powerful work of Jesus) as we see it in the glimpses we have of the early Church, both in the account in Acts and through Paul's letters; and in what the Church has experienced ever since then. And is still experiencing today. For we begin to see the characteristic qualities of the new life in the Spirit, which we noted as given at Pentecost to the gathered disciples, becoming the hallmark of Christians, both individually and as communities. So much so that Paul is able to challenge the young churches whenever these fruits of the Spirit are lacking. And this challenge remains one we must take to ourselves most seriously as we approach the Millennium.

For just as Pentecost was an event which made the disparate group of believers one *ecclesia* (church) united in a common witness to the world, so his making the disparate into one continues to be a primary work of the Holy Spirit. Unity is one of the key gifts of the Spirit, because in unity (not uniformity) a new life is created, the life of believers 'together'. That is why disunity among Christians is such an offence: it is a rejection of that gift, and of the powerful new life which can only flow from it. We see the signs of this very early in the young Church's life. For there is in Acts first of all a moving account of how the unity of the first Christians was so great that they shared all goods in common, as a material expression of the worship they shared. The Spirit had brought them a common vision, a common bond in their faith in Jesus Christ, and a common experience of the power of God. Out of this grew a common concern for those in need, so that through their shared care 'there were no needy persons among them' (Acts 4:34). So when this unity was betrayed, the consequences were awesome; indeed they were mortal. That is the point of the terrible story of Ananias and Sapphira, whose offence was not that they kept back money, but that they pretended to be united in this common commitment when in fact they were not. And so by their lies they were destroying the unity of the gathering. And since that unity was not of human devising, but of the Spirit's giving, they were betraying that gift and lying to God himself (Acts 5:1–11). The terror of that was real: so real that they died of it; so real that 'great fear seized the whole church and all who heard about these events'.

I have spent time on this because it is not possible to overstate how vital is this gift by the Spirit of 'unity', how far from any human devising, how potent with divine power. The word *koinonia* (fellowship) used widely in the New Testament for this gift to the Church, describing the bond its members shared in their faith, is seen by Paul as a mark of the way the Church shares the life of the Godhead. He concludes, for instance, his second letter to the Corinthians, 'The grace of the Lord Jesus Christ, and the love of God, and the fellowship [sharing in] of the Holy Spirit be with you all.' So anything which would threaten that unity – sectarian attitudes, élitist assumptions, selfishness and intellectual pride – is the subject of Paul's strongest condemnation (1 Corinthians 1:12; 3:1; 6:19; 8:1 – to note but one letter!). For these things are seen as elements which break fellowship, destroying not only immediacy of communion but the precious gift of fuller participation in the life of the Godhead itself; and loss of living in God's power follows. In our own day we can only reflect in profound penitence on the sad history of the Church, up to and including the history we are ourselves making, in the brokenness of that gift of unity through human wilfulness and sin. Fractured as that unity is, we nevertheless have all experienced something of the gift of *koinonia*; enough for us to long to recover it more fully. Enough for us to work unceasingly to do so; not only for the sake of the Church, but even more for the world to which the Church in its God-given unity was intended as a blessing, a mirror of the life within the Godhead itself and a channel of the undivided love that is God's.

For we within the Church often forget that the work of the Spirit continues unceasingly outside the Church, in the world. *Ubi caritas et amor, Deus ibi est* – where there is charity and love, there God is – is a chant emanating from Taizé and sung all over the world, including at the World Council of Churches Assembly, gathered in all its unity and disunity. Where God is, there is the Spirit, at work within that very love and charity. So in our receiving of the gift of unity in the Spirit we need to be alert to how we may discern him at work in the world as well as within the Christian community.

2. THE GIFT OF POWER

It is a weak doctrine of the Spirit which ducks the truth that the early Church as we know it through the New Testament had a most confident conviction of the Spirit's power at work within it. The expectation of the first Christians was that God would act in power in spite of the Christian community's vulnerability through persecution or opposition or sheer lack of social clout, or through its own internal weakness of misunderstandings and even heresy. They were quite sure that prayers would be answered powerfully, and that the work of the gospel would go from strength to strength.

Today we in the Church often disclaim any such confident assertion, on the grounds sometimes of fear of triumphalism. Apart from the fact that our witness is often so weak that triumphalism is about the last charge that could be made against us(!), this anxiety disregards the nature of that early Christian confidence. For the New Testament teaching about the gift by the Spirit of power to Christ's followers is firmly anchored in the real world of human weakness and sinfulness. The same Church in which this power was shown included the sinfulness of

Ananias and Sapphira and the strength of Stephen. He suffered martyrdom in the power of the Spirit (not a power in worldly terms) and the Spirit indeed enabled him to glimpse Christ in the glory and power of heaven itself, and in that same power, forgive those who were murdering him. Paul himself is an example of this power in the midst of human weakness; for the same Paul who achieves the mighty ministry to the Gentiles in the power of the Spirit is the Paul who pleads unavailingly to be freed of the mysterious 'thorn in the flesh' which distresses him. This leads him to an insight from the Lord himself: 'My power is made perfect in weakness' (2 Corinthians 12:9). In Christian history, as in contemporary experience, weakness is invariably the soil in which the power of God, mediated by the Spirit, is most fully and gloriously demonstrated.

Characteristics of life in the Spirit

The presence of the Spirit in the life and ministry of Jesus means, as we have seen, that he was involved in that process of the redemption of Creation which God was effecting through Jesus. That is, he was and is present in the experience of believers as they were and are re-created in the likeness of Jesus. It follows, as one theologian recently put it, that the Spirit's work – his 'mission' – is 'to form a Christ-like humanity', not just 'simply spread about sensations of the transcendent'. To create, that is, the relationships which constitute the kingdom of God, not to nurture individual religious intensity.

What are the hallmarks of that 'Christ-like humanity' thus being created through the decades since the coming of the Spirit at Pentecost, and the relationships that new humanity enjoys which constitute the kingdom of God?

Clearly the unity and dynamic power which we've noted as the primary work of the Spirit among believers help create these, but how do they show themselves?

Frequently we find reference, in Acts and in Paul's letters, to the gifts (*charismata*) of the Spirit. Some of the more overt and dramatic ones, such as 'speaking in tongues', clearly attracted considerable misunderstanding even in the early Church – as they have done throughout the Church's long history. So much so that what was properly given for the unity and powerful effectiveness of the Church's life, instead has become at times the cause of division and a blunting of her mission.

Yet the New Testament is quite clear that, within a church which is living out, in the unity and power of the Spirit, a continuation of Jesus' ministry, there is no distinction between those who have the more overt and dramatic *charismata* and those whose *charismata* are hidden and behind the scenes. All Christians receive the *charis*, grace – that is, unmerited blessing – of the Spirit, and that grace will show itself in their lives and service in a variety of ways. In 1 Corinthians 12:4–11, 27–31 and Ephesians 4:4–6, for instance, we find lists of the profusion of gifts currently found within the Church's ministry at the time of writing. We do not now even know what all of them precisely were. All we can say is that the New Testament shows awareness of the richness of the Spirit's gifts, and the 'untidiness' of the description perhaps is salutary in shaming our own liking for 'order' at the expense of 'life'.

If the gifts of the Spirit are to help create the relationships which constitute the kingdom of God, it follows that their purpose is primarily not for the one receiving the gift, but the building up of the community of believers. So, for instance, Paul points to the relative merits of the gift of tongues (*glossalalia*) and prophecy. Both are true gifts of the Spirit, and to be rejoiced in. But speaking in tongues has the primary effect of building up the individual's life in the Spirit, whereas prophecy edifies the whole congregation (1 Corinthians 14:4). Therefore, he urges, long for those gifts which are for the good of others. Above all he urges reverence and yearning, therefore, for the gift of *caritas*, holy love, because it is for the building up of others, often at the expense of ourselves. Holy love is in fact the dynamic of those relationships which constitute the kingdom of God. It is the very hallmark of a Christlike humanity.

However, the word 'holy' reminds us of an essential feature of the Spirit's life and work in and through the Trinity of which he is part. He is the 'Holy' Spirit, and wherever he is, there is present the gift of holiness; where he is not, there is the ugliness of sin and all the opposites of holiness that scar God's wonderful Creation. The Holy Spirit creates holy communities; his work in us as individuals is to continue the work of sanctification which commences with our baptism or conversion in Christ and goes on to the fullness of life in Christ. How astonishing in my day that holiness is so rarely spoken of and so often mocked as if it is the realm of soft people who live in disapproving separation from the world. I hope that in your time, my dear future friends, you will have recovered from this polarisation between holiness and strength. Holiness, you see, is not weakness. On the contrary, it involves discipline, sacrifice; and sometimes it will take the sacrifice of everything to challenge evil and sin. Indeed, rather than separating us from the world, holiness will at times thrust us right into the centre of the conflict, to suffer for truth. For that matter, there is nothing soft about the monks and nuns who have for the sake of the gospel withdrawn from the world in order to pray for the world. Nothing is more compelling as Christian witness than those who live lives which shine out for God; which proclaim that integrity and purity of life are possible when we surrender to the Holy Spirit. Neither is there anything *moralistic* about the Spirit's work. The command to 'be holy as I am holy' is not something we do in our own power or for our own sake. Christianity is not a rule-book religion. No: the gospel is about a holy God who pours his Spirit into weak people to make them holy; who gives us the power to be 'good'; who empowers his people with such a desire and affection for God that it is our joy to please him and our pleasure to do the things that he desires for us.

Aspects of the Trinity

It is because of the Church's experience of such life of the Spirit, in its many forms and through its many gifts, that while Paul never develops a systematic doctrine of the Trinity, the shape of one is beginning to emerge in the New Testament. There is no gainsaying the astonishing number of verses which speak of a 'threeness' in the unity of God. For instance, 'There are different kinds of gifts, but *the same Spirit* [*pneuma*]. There are different kinds of service, but *the same Lord* [*kurios*]. There are different kinds of working, but *the same God* [*theos*] works all of them in all men' (1 Corinthians 12:4–6, my italics). And again, 'One Spirit . . . one Lord . . . one God' (Ephesians 4:4–6); '*God* sent the *Spirit* of his *Son* into our hearts' (Galatians 4:6, my italics); 'Peter . . . to God's elect . . . who have been chosen according to the foreknowledge of *God the Father* through the sanctifying work of *the Spirit* for obedience to *Jesus Christ*' (1 Peter 1:2, my italics). While Paul never abandons his monotheism, there is a 'threeness' about his experience of God which is much more than simply three experiences of one God. The divinity of Christ and the divinity of the Spirit were, of course, to find careful formulation in the later doctrine of the Trinity.

But how can this formulation of a doctrine help us? What do we actually gain in our Christian lives because of it? Perhaps we might find a story helps us here.

Years ago, I worked in an office in London. The director of the branch was to me an awesome man, austere, remote and not given to humour. Once a day he swept through the main office with scarcely a word to anyone, and he was rarely to be seen thereafter, although occasionally a voice raised in anger was heard emanating from the oak-lined room, and sometimes juniors would emerge ashen white from his presence. No one could doubt that the branch was well run; but it was run on fear.

One day I fell foul of the director. I was instructed to go to a certain shop for him, and buy a gift for someone. I was given £5 but on the way I lost it; and it was an awful lot of money in those days! To say I was terrified was to put it mildly. At the age of sixteen such a calamity seemed irredeemable. I had to go to him and tell him what I had done. He sat behind his desk and his face seemed to get darker and darker as my tale unfolded. Then he said, 'You have failed. How are you going to make good the loss?' I gulped, and I think I replied, 'Well, sir, I expect the money to be taken from my wages [at that time £2.50 a week] and I will try to do better.' Then the revelation. A flicker of a smile came across his face. He softened. He reached into his wallet and pulled out another £5 note and said, 'Let's try again, shall we? Get that gift and report back.' Clutching that note as if it were the Crown Jewels I went off to complete my errand. On return he asked me to sit down, and then he asked me about my education. From that meeting he took a daily interest in my reading, and to that man I owe my love of literature.

The point is that it took a personal encounter – and one in which I was exposed and open to him – to discover the deeper truth about the kind of boss I had; and from that moment on he became to me much more than simply a remote and feared figure. He became a friend. Now all analogies are inexact, and I am certainly not suggesting that the fear of God is like that, but the Christian experience has certain parallels with that story. For in it God – the feared and awesome God – encounters his people through new disclosures of himself, as he reveals himself to them in the way particular events and contexts make appropriate. In the Bible these disclosures are seen to centre around three mighty acts of God: creating, saving and inspiring. And in all three not only is the Person of Christ definitive, but all three Persons are involved in the divine disclosure: the Spirit in interpreting the mighty acts of God through Christ, and actualising creation, salvation and inspiration within us. The linear view of the work of God (as Father creating, then Son saving, then Spirit inspiring or sanctifying) could tempt us to a view of what is technically known as the 'divine economy' (the work of creation and salvation) in which each of the Persons of the Godhead 'take their turn'. In fact what understanding God as Trinity does for us is to help us recognise that in each mighty act of God there is no division of Person, but all are equally involved. So that, for instance, at the event of Pentecost it is 'the power of God the Father' and the 'grace of God the Son, Jesus Christ' which comes upon the disciples in the fire and wind of the Spirit.

We see this particularly clearly in Paul's account in Romans 8, where, as the Doctrine Commission put it, he describes how 'believers are caught up into the life of the Godhead through the Spirit, incorporated into the Son, with the firm and assured status of children by adoption, enabled therefore to join in the Son's ceaseless prayer of "Abba" to the Father'.

Implications for Christians today

'Enabled therefore to join in the Son's ceaseless prayer . . .' Here we begin to touch on one of the profound implications for us now, of the truth that God is triune. For *because* God is the Three-in-One, his ceaseless activity, whether we are engaging with him or not, is of *responding* as well as offering. And to be invited to be a Christlike humanity is therefore to be drawn to a particular calling in the world – one of ceaseless offering and receiving; one of reciprocation. For we are drawn in prayer into a 'conversation' constantly ongoing within the Godhead. That is, we not only *cannot* pray alone, but are never required to: our prayers are always part of the mutuality between Father, Son and Spirit. That is why Paul is able to speak of the Spirit praying in and with us: 'We do not know what we ought to pray for, but the Spirit himself intercedes for us with groans that words cannot express. And he who searches our hearts *knows the mind of the Spirit*, because the Spirit intercedes for the saints in accordance with God's will' (Romans 8:26–27, my italics). And part of our calling in the world is to offer this being drawn into the mind of God, by the Spirit, for the world.

In the strength and power of this life of prayer rooted, so to speak, in the ceaseless relationship of love within the Trinity, whose vibrations we catch sometimes as we pray, we are able to hold some of the characteristics of the life of the Spirit over against the pressures of our culture.

For instance, how does the abundance of God which overflows through Christ Jesus and which is characteristic of the giving of the Spirit (we noticed it in the events of Pentecost) – how does that 'ecology of blessing' confront our present Western culture of excess? May it not be that for our own generation, overwhelmed by information, busyness, boredom, anxieties, problems, stimuli, material goods, drugs, instant communication, fast money, fast talk and fast food, the Holy Spirit within the Trinity offers to us 'divine' excess? The Early Fathers of the Church talked of 'sober intoxication'. The letter to the Ephesians urges that we be 'filled with the Spirit', not drunk with wine. We know for ourselves, as communities of believers, the Holy Spirit as the self-distribution of the abundance of God. Is not this something which we should be offering to our world as our own experience of that characteristic life in the Spirit which diverts us from the needless and heedless and destructive life of excess, into the profound and satisfying abundance of life as God has created, redeemed and sanctified it through Christ?

And again, each aspect of the 'fruit of the Spirit' – love, joy, peace, patience, kindness, goodness, faithfulness, gentleness, humility – are these not prophetic to our culture? Do they not stand over against the values implicit – and indeed often grievingly explicit – in newsprint, in magazines and journals and TV programmes which glorify violence, casual lust, competition, human beings as objects to possess, confrontation, and endless judgementalism and scapegoating? That boldness, i.e. courage, which characterised the stand made and the words spoken publicly in the power of the Spirit and the name of Jesus by those early Christians – is not that same courage and boldness equally available to us *today*, in the

Spirit and in the name of Jesus, were we to ask for it as we engage in the public forum on these very issues, presenting the divine alternatives life-giving to a society?

And further, our understanding of a triune God engages with issues concerning our existence in our physical world. For the triune God is not a 'God of the gaps', but God of the whole process of the physical universe. Current scientific thinking allows for openness and flexibility of physical possibility. The process of the world, it has been suggested by a well-known scientist–theologian, Sir John Polkinghorne, is not just 'the inexorable unwinding of a gigantic piece of cosmic clockwork', but rather its possibilities are open, 'so that a genuine "becoming" takes place, yielding actual novelty. In that case the possibility of some interaction between creation and the Creator-Spirit seems an appropriate expectation. Much scientific understanding of the nature of the physical world is by no means inhospitable to this view.' The 'interactedness' of the life of the Trinity supports this perspective of openness and flexibility.

The suffering God

But for me the most profound impact of all of an understanding of God as Trinity, is the way it is possible to discover him as a God who, far from being impervious to the suffering of his Creation, shares it. It was the famous theologian Jürgen Moltmann who suggested that we could only talk about God's suffering in Trinitarian terms. Why was it that the early Christian Fathers so stoutly maintained the principle of God's 'incapacity for suffering', although in worship Christians adored the crucified Christ as God, and so in preaching often spoke of God's suffering? They saw God's freedom from suffering as a fundamental distinction between himself and his Creation, subject as all creatures were to suffering, transience and death. Salvation therefore meant for them sharing in God's eternal unsuffering life, sharing his freedom from change and the mourning that often attends it.

Moltmann points out that this suggests only two alternatives: either 'impassibility' – an essential incapacity to suffer – or a fateful subjection to it, such as all created beings know. But the Trinitarian understanding of God offers a third alternative: that of divinely chosen suffering, actively entered upon. The choice voluntarily to be affected by another: a choice for which the dynamic must be – can only be – passionate love. Love such as is ceaselessly offered and received between the three Persons of the Trinity.

The key to this is the *voluntariness* of God the Father's suffering, through his Son, within the agency of the Spirit. It was the early Christian scholar Origen who perhaps first pointed to this understanding. He talked of the divine passion which Christ suffers for us, and at the same time he pointed to a divine passion between the Father and the Son, interpreted and conveyed through the Spirit. That is, the divine suffering of love outwards, towards us and the whole Creation, was grounded in the pain of love within and among the three Persons of the Trinity.

These are great mysteries, and we can but glimpse in them something of the wonder of the God whose love is poured out ceaselessly as part of his very nature. Such meditations bring us finally to the very essence of the issue, that which all these Letters, my dear friends of the future, have really been about. Quite simply: What is God like?

What is God like?

It was William Temple who once remarked, 'The wise question is not, "Is Christ divine?", but "What is God like?"' And this question lies at the heart of the doctrine of the Trinity. The New Testament answer to the question is clear.

First, to know what God is like we need look no further than his Son. 'No-one has ever seen God, but God the One and Only, who is at the Father's side, has made him known' (John 1:18); 'Anyone who has seen me has seen the Father' (John 14:9b). And then, in Jesus God is revealed, through the help of the Holy Spirit, to be a God whose love overflows in power and forgiveness to save his people.

Moreover, through Jesus the fatherhood of God is revealed, and through the Holy Spirit the Son is revealed. The Spirit is the one through whom we understand the wonders of God, and are enabled to make them our own.

Finally, it is through the Spirit that we are able to accept the power of the Cross and the Resurrection into our lives, thus becoming 'a new creation'. It is the Spirit who maintains us in our living for God, and in the praying which sustains it.

And this fourfold New Testament answer helps us to see the strength of the doctrine of the Trinity: it unites the doctrine of the *nature* of God with the doctrine of the *work* of God. What the New Testament writers realised implicitly and the later Church expressed explicitly is that unless the work of salvation connects deeply and personally with God himself, there is no salvation worth speaking of. ***Jesus Christ is only the Saviour of the world if he is in some utterly true sense God.*** The acts of Jesus in his life, death and resurrection are only saving acts if they are divine acts. Unless there is a relation of oneness in nature between the divine Father and the man Jesus, then the foundation of our salvation collapses. And we must say the same of the Spirit. He, in nature one with Father and Son, applies the work of salvation to our hearts, he intercedes in sighs too deep for words, he pours the love of God into our hearts . . . he is the agent of God's abundance of gifts to us.

Yet we are not talking of three Gods but of one, in whom three Persons are eternally present to and with each other, eternally interacting in the pouring out of divine love for the creating and saving and sanctifying of the Creation, each present within the activity and work of the other.

So the doctrine of the Trinity expresses what every Christian knows intuitively. It seeks to put into human language what is actually beyond human language, for the inner workings of God are ultimately inexpressible. 'A doctrine is that which hedges about a mystery,' said St Augustine. But the hedge is needed to help us glimpse at least in outline the wonder of the nature and work of Almighty God in his care for us.

That care covers the vastness of Creation through space and time. So it is to that final mystery, the mystery of the Last Things, that we must now turn. And of that I shall speak in my next – and last – Letter.

Yours in thankfulness for the gracious mystery of the Trinity,

LETTER 10

'And God Shall Be All in All'

Dear Friends of the Future,

And now we come, finally, to think together about that marvellous hope which transcends time, and which therefore binds together all past Christians with those of my own generation and you of the future; so that because of it, 'we may merrily meet in Heaven'. For 'your kingdom come' is the prayer to God, through the ages, of the whole Christian Church. And while this prayer has reference to affairs of this life (for the faith of Jesus Christ is rooted in the world and seeks to change people and institutions) yet it more profoundly looks beyond the things that are, to the final and consummated coming of the kingdom of God. Indeed, one of the ways in which the New Testament most deeply challenges us in this century – and, I suspect, in yours – is that through its entirety it throbs with the confident expectation of the Second Coming of Christ and the final redemption of the world. This almost-beyond-imagining consummation beyond time and space is conceived of as in some way including the universe, in a new heaven and earth, though – to quote Mr Spock – earth, 'but not as we know it'. Traditional theology speaks of the Four Last Things: death, judgement, hell and heaven in a context in which this world and its ultimate destiny, and that of its inhabitants, are part of something much vaster. Of this the early Church was entirely confident.

But in what sense is it possible for contemporary Christians to speak, from a wholly different culture and from its current technical understanding of the universe, with any certainty at all about such an expectation – apart from the one perceived inevitability: that of death? What does our faith affirm even today about our ultimate future on the other side not only of our own individual deaths, but that of the earth itself, indeed the very universe itself?

The characteristic mood of most intelligent Western people is, as our century closes, at bottom one of pessimism concerning the future, whether of individuals or of the world. Such pessimism is understandable in the context of our climate of religious agnosticism or even straight disbelief. For, thus naked, we face the implications of philosophies insisting on the essential 'randomness' of life, the tiny human species caught in a struggle for survival within a pitiless and amoral universe. And the scale of that universe has been revealed as far vaster than we had conceived, with our own planet insignificant within a small galaxy which is but one of galaxies without number. Inevitably we are driven to wonder whether anything concerning our own puny existence has any meaning or value at all, let alone an eternal one.

Moreover, distinguished scientists have confirmed the certain end of the universe, in either bang or whimper. As John Polkinghorne has put it:

When cosmologists think about the ultimate fate of the universe, they conclude that it is going to end badly. A gigantic tug-of-war is going on between two opposing cosmic principles. One is the expansive force of the Big Bang, blowing the galaxies apart. The other is the contractive force of gravity, pulling them together. These two tendencies are almost in balance, and we cannot tell which will gain the ultimate upper hand. If expansion ultimately prevails, the galaxies will continue to recede from each other forever. Within each galaxy, however, gravity will certainly win, and the galaxies will condense into gigantic black holes that will in time decay into low-grade radiation. If that is the future scenario, the universe will end in a whimper. The prospect is no less bleak if gravity prevails. In that case, the present expansion will one day be halted and reversed. What began with the Big Bang will end in the Big Crunch, as the whole world falls back into a cosmic melting pot. That way, the universe ends in a bang. Either way, it is condemned to futility.

If that is not enough to persuade humankind that there is no meaning and no enduring hope, we have only to add the moral and physical history of our world, where there is not only innocent suffering and evil triumphant over long periods, but dreadful cataclysms in the natural world to which creatures including humanity fall victim; where there are disasters natural and man-made; where power is the ultimate goal, and the vulnerable and weaker become but the means to an end. So that whether the immediate cause of suffering is inherent in the natural world, through disease or natural disaster, or whether it is in what humankind has made of its life in the world, crushing the helpless under its juggernaut of self-seeking, the grounds for belief in the ultimate victory of 'the good' seem to many people, as a matter of integrity, to be suspect and unwarranted. As Helen Oppenheimer once put it, 'People who preach a felicity which outsoars the agonies of humanity can appear worse than shallow.'

Therefore, although our century began on a wave of optimism, and has seen astonishing social and scientific developments which have greatly enhanced the quality of life for millions, yet as this century ends no grand ideological vision seizes human imagination. Rather there are doom eschatologies around no less startling than the Bible's account of the end of all things (which itself resonates with the soberly thoughtful cosmological conclusion offered by Polkinghorne above). There are those who believe that our failure to control human greed, acquisitiveness and even the world population, will result in environmental catastrophe, ending in starvation, disease and extinction. There are those who predict that some such developments will lead inevitably to a third world war. Unsurprisingly, they expect this to be a war in which we exterminate ourselves as a species. There is yet a third 'doom eschatology' which predicts that on 14th August 2026 Comet Swift/Tuttle will collide with our planet wiping out all life, as it is argued a similar comet's collision destroyed so many species 65 million years ago. Such scenarios would put in question even your existence, my dear friends of the future, let alone hope beyond that.

It is in the context of such anxieties, such lack of hope and such fears about the future, both personal and universal, that we turn to look again at what the Christian faith affirms. The calm and assured message of the Bible does not disregard the realities of which these fears are the expression. But in facing them and interpreting them, it assures us that whatever the future holds, *God is*, and is, as Bishop David Jenkins used to say, 'as he is in Jesus'. The Christian hope does not depend on an almanac which gives us a date when Christ will return in victory; but it insists that we may rely on it. He *will* return. There *will be* an establishing in totality of his kingdom of love, light and justice, the mode of which can only be glimpsed in picture language. For beyond the Four Last Things – death so familiar and so unyielding, judgement so feared and rebelled against, hell expressing all that is ultimately most negative and destructive, and heaven, that dream of high delight in the immediate presence of God to be enjoyed for ever – beyond even these is the *Last Thing* of all, on which all depends: the immortal and eternal God.

> There, in that other world, what waits for me?
> What shall I find after that other birth?
> No stormy, tossing, foaming sea,
>   But a new earth.
>
> No sun to mark the changing of the days,
> No slow, soft falling of the alternate night,
> No moon, no star, no light upon my ways,
>   Only the Light.
>
> No gray cathedral, wide and wondrous fair,
> That I may tread where all my fathers trod,
> Nay, nay, my soul, no house of God is there,
>   But only God.
>
> *Mary Coleridge*

And that is why it is vital that as Christians we do not surrender to the seduction of dark unbelief, or even its timid brother, a diffident agnosticism which shrugs off the hard question with a 'who can tell?' defence, attempting to side-step equally the nihilism of unbelief and the painful wrestling with reality of faith. The social and personal consequences of either avoiding the issue or surrendering to unbelief are incalculable. For where there is no faith, there is no hope for a future; where there is no hope, there is no reaching out after God, no grasping the securities that rest in his nature; and ultimately without him, there is nothing at all. As I have said repeatedly during my time as Archbishop, without God there can be no absolute values on which to depend.

And that is why it is a matter of concern, not only for us at the end of the second millennium, but for you who are to come, that our culture's despairing conclusions have had some impact even on our Christian perceptions, depriving them of the confidence they could rightly have, not by ignoring the realities with which we are confronted, but by steadily looking through them at the God whose faithfulness our own faith attests. And such loss of confidence has inevitably led to unsure and tentative teaching and preaching, a pale shadow to hand on to you of the robust and full-blooded faith handed on to us. Indeed, eschatology – that doctrine of hope which names the Last Things – is among the most neglected themes of Christian preaching in the West today. And that has resulted not only in the impoverishment of the Church, but in a failure, we must acknowledge with shame, to address the hunger and the spiritual wounds of our age. Yet such attenuation of the faith is unnecessary. I myself have witnessed time and again the truth that where the Church is confident in its doctrine of God 'making all things new', it is strong in its mission and sense of well-being. There, for instance, in the heroic Church of Sudan, facing privation of unimaginable poverty, suffering and rootlessness; there, in the courageous Anglican Church of Mozambique, facing the challenge of post-colonial changes and opposition to Christianity – in both places, and many more besides, a living faith in the Lord of the future inspires evangelism and church growth.

For the Church to be true to itself and its Lord, a recovery of nerve is vital, a rediscovery of what God's promise of his eternal kingdom is, and of how we may glimpse it in understanding, in the very context of those pressures which would seem to destroy its credibility. I hope that my own generation will, belatedly, make that rediscovery, and so pass it on to you richly, not by evading the challenge of the thought and the scientific knowledge of our times, but by engaging with them, in the light of a sure faith in the nature of God himself, the Father of our Lord Jesus Christ. But if we fail, then it will be for you, my dear friends of the future, to set right any lack in the faith we hand on, and most particularly in respect of God's commitment of himself concerning our future.

An eschatology of hope

In times past, the emphases of the Christian eschatology of hope have differed according to the nature of those times. When oppression and disaster have filled life with a sense of imminent crisis, the hope of God's final, determinative action is that there should be an entirely fresh start: as our Doctrine Commission recently succinctly summarised it, the focus of apocalyptic hope in such times is, 'Let God begin again!' At quieter and more peaceful periods, the hope associated with 'the End' is more in terms of renewal of an old and weary world: 'Let the coming end of the tired world prove a new beginning in God.' In either case reflection about the End Time is rooted in two things: the Biblical promise of God, 'Behold, I make all things new'; and the faithfulness which is an essential attribute of God's nature. Because he is the kind of God he is, we may trust his promise. And that promise is insistently one of a future of hope for

Creation, and most specifically, for humankind within Creation.

As I pointed out in Letter 5 it is now some little time since scholars demonstrated that the End Time, as a promise rather than a threat, was *absolutely central* to the message of Jesus, as proclaimed not only in his teaching and stories but in his life and his death and his rising again. The apocalyptic expectations of his day provided Jesus with the language and imagery for what was the wholly new promise which was the very essence of his mission. There could be no separation, therefore, of the faith in the incarnate Jesus from the future coming of Jesus; no separation of saving faith now from faith in the eternal life to come. While in due course the early Church's expectation of Christ's Second Coming as 'imminent' necessarily gave way to a changed perception of time-scale, this in no way altered the centrality, within the Christian faith, of the promise for our ultimate destiny with God and the hope therefore running through even the most traumatic vision of the Last Things.

The breadth and depth of this ultimate hope is vast, for it looks beyond all that is imaginable in time and space and what may happen 'when the heavens crumple like a garment', and yet it draws that vastness and universality into the local particularity that is the everyday living of you and me. For the promise of eternity of life to those who love him, beyond time, is for this life also, here and now, where immortality qualitatively begins. This New Testament truth – that the eternal life which is our hope begins here and now, as the Fourth Gospel repeatedly reminds us – is one of the most helpful ways of approaching, as we now must, the first of the Four Last Things which are the Bible's signposts to the mystery of our ultimate future.

Death

I vividly recall my first sight of a dead person: it was when I was a young clergyman. I called on the family to make the arrangements for the funeral of a beloved old lady who had been a faithful member of our congregation, and her sister invited me to view her body. To this day I remember the sense of shock and disbelief as I saw the hollow, grey, wizened shell where once had lived a dear and loving person. To be sure it was her body, but it was certainly not the person I knew. As I looked, the sheer truth of her absence from that place seized me, and the words of the angel at the Lord's tomb interpreted that absence for me as they flashed into my mind: 'He is not here; he is risen.' I knew then my fellow Christian was not there, but with her Lord. And I also at that moment entered much more fully into the 'emptiness' of death (which is its aspect which most fills us with grief and horror) and what it meant that Christ had put a bridge across that emptiness so that it could have no ultimate terror for us.

For death calls into question any ultimate meaning to our life, this precious and mysterious gift which our strongest instincts make us cling to. It makes it seem as Shakespeare so finely said,

> a tale told by an idiot
> Full of sound and fury, signifying nothing.

We rebel against its intractable reality because we so often experience it as the frustration of all our hopes and love. Death seems a denial of our highest ideals. This is not simply our powerful physical reaction to it – the horror of warm and living flesh encountering the cold physical reality of the corpse. More deeply, it is our sense that *this is not what we were made for.* As the haunting words of Ecclesiastes 3:11 put it: 'He has ... set eternity in the hearts of men; yet they cannot fathom what God has done from beginning to end.'

The Bible's way of understanding death helps us to grapple with both its physical and spiritual desolation. It considers death from two points of view. First, it sees its annihilating power – its tyranny of 'absentness' – as 'the wages of sin' (Romans 5:12), an inherent consequence of the rejection by humankind of life lived according to God's direction. (Genesis 3 is a profound narrative exploration of this theology.) We do not, that is, fear death only because we fear the nothingness of physical dissolution, or our loss and bereavement of those most dear to us. We fear it for ourselves also because at bottom we shrink from entering, with all our waywardness clogging our steps, the mystery of the immediate presence of a holy God. That this profounder fear is as real today as in the past, but inarticulate and unformulated, was visibly shown in that map of the mid-century, Beckett's *Waiting for Godot*. One revealing conversation between the two tramps who are its chief characters runs thus:

VLADIMIR: Two thieves, crucified at the same time as our Saviour. One –
ESTRAGON: Our what?
VLADIMIR: Our Saviour. Two thieves. One is supposed to have been saved and the other . . . (he searches for the contrary of saved) . . . damned.
ESTRAGON: Saved from what?
VLADIMIR: Hell.
ESTRAGON: I'm going. (he does not move)
VLADIMIR: And yet . . . how is it that of the four Evangelists only one speaks of a thief being saved? The four of them were there – or thereabouts – and only one of them speaks

of a thief being saved . . . One out of the four. Of the other three two don't mention any thieves at all, and the third says that both of them abused him.

ESTRAGON: Who?

VLADIMIR: What?

ESTRAGON: What's all this about? Abused who?

VLADIMIR: The Saviour.

ESTRAGON: Why?

VLADIMIR: Because he wouldn't save them.

ESTRAGON: From hell?

VLADIMIR: Imbecile! From death.

ESTRAGON: I thought you said hell.

VLADIMIR: From death, from death. . . .

I wonder if it is true of your time as it is of mine that often we can only talk about serious things by holding them in the context of dark humour as Beckett does in that passage. Another writer and comedian of my time, Woody Allen, a Jewish actor tortured by the theme of death, once said: 'Death? I'm not afraid of dying. I simply do not want to be around when it happens.'

But we *shall* be around when our deaths happen; and that takes us back, my dear friends of the future, to the wonder of the work of Christ for us which, as I pointed out in a previous letter, addresses not only our present sense of helpless sinfulness, but also our fear of this primary Last Thing, death itself, at the very deepest level. For God has delivered his people from sin, and therefore also from the deepest consequences of death. As the writers of *The Mystery of Salvation* recently reminded us, on the other side of this feared Last Thing lie, because of Christ's work for us, freedom from that sacred terror, and hope in the face of annihilation: 'Salvation, liberation, deliverance will come on the Day of the Lord, when his righteous judgement will triumph, his will at last be done, and the dead will be raised to life.' And this is so because the Day of the Lord is to be ushered in by the coming to us again of the same Lord Jesus Christ who loved us and gave his life that we might no longer have any need to fear death.

But what of the 'resurrection of the body'? In other words, how does the Bible confront the reality and mystery of physical dissolution? Its second perspective on death helps us here. It presents it as the inevitable physical end of all living things: a part of the given pattern. And indeed our own palaeontologists have shown us that the physical fact of death was the rule long before Homo Sapiens appeared on the scene. The fact of physical death has not changed as a reality for Creation. What has changed for us in the West is the weight we give that fact. Our predecessors in the faith, taught by the Bible and their experience of God which confirmed that teaching, looked beyond the physical fact in hope of God's promises for eternity. Contemporary humankind, out of touch with spiritual realities, sees nothing but blank dissolution.

And this sense of the relentless fact of ultimate dissolution applies, as we have seen, not simply to us as individual physical entities, but to our world and all its creatures, and to the very universe itself. How may we respond as Christians to this fear?

Recently our Church of England Doctrine Commission took up this very point, recognising that the issue was of the redemption of 'matter'. And they began from the Biblical insistence that not just in our finite world, but in the eternal perspective of the creating God, 'Matter matters'. Mortal transience is indeed the necessary cost of new life within the processes by which we are currently bound. (They argue that an evolving universe allowed by

its Creator to explore and realise its God-given potentiality cannot be otherwise, since it has been given by God the
freedom to be itself, existing in chosen separateness from
him.) But the Bible is emphatic that beyond death there is
another existence, in a 'body' – what other word will do?
– unimaginable to us but in a real sense 'material'. As John
Polkinghorne, the scientist from whom I quoted earlier,
has put it: 'The laws of nature of that first creation were
those that were appropriate to such a world, allowed to
realise its own potentiality. The new creation will be
something different; it is a creation *ex vetere*, for it is the
transmutation of the old consequent upon its free return
to its Creator.'

That's it! That is what Jesus Christ has done. He has
blessed 'matter' as we know it by his incarnate life on
earth. But far more profoundly even than that, because he
submitted that material life to a willing obedience to his
Father, our God, all material life has made its 'free return'
to its God, in him. Because he submitted that material life
in willing and loving obedience, even to the processes of
death itself, death, even physical death as we know it,
even the dissolution of the universe as we predict it, is
caught up in the pattern of eternal and unquenchable life
which is the will of God for his Creation.

And that is why Paul can – and must – talk with absolute
conviction not simply of the life of eternity but of the 'body'
in which that life will be experienced. For, 'By this gospel,'
he declares, 'you are saved . . . if Christ has not been raised,
our preaching is useless and so is your faith . . . if Christ has
not been raised, your faith is futile; you are still in your
sins. Then those also who have fallen asleep [=died] in
Christ are lost. If only for this life we have hope in Christ,
we are to be pitied more than all men' (1 Corinthians 15:2,
14, 17–19). And he goes on to explore the question someone

will ask, 'With what kind of body will the dead be raised?'
A 'body' – 'matter' – as different in form, Paul says, from
the one we presently know, as our present human bodies
differ not only from the animals, fish and birds, but from
the 'heavenly bodies' of sun and stars.

> So it will be with the resurrection of the dead. The body that
> is sown is perishable, it is raised imperishable; it is sown in
> dishonour, it is raised in glory; it is sown in weakness, it is
> raised in power; it is sown a natural body, it is raised a spiri-
> tual body. . . . And just as we have borne the likeness of the
> earthly man, so shall we bear the likeness of the man from
> heaven. . . . For the trumpet will sound, the dead will be
> raised imperishable, and we will be changed. . . . When the
> perishable has been clothed with the imperishable, and the
> mortal with immortality, then the saying that is written will
> come true: 'Death has been swallowed up in victory!' (1
> Corinthians 15:42–44, 49, 52, 54)

And for my generation, with its raised consciousness
about the preservation of the earth, and its awareness of
the predicted end of the universe, that paean of confident
praise refers also to a glorious new, wholly changed but
still recognisable life of a universe which has become for
us a 'cosmos', making ultimate sense of its history, the
'new heaven and the new earth' of the book of Revelation;
as well as to the resurrection life of each individual.

The practice of the promise of rescue

For the first Christians this discovery that death was
defeated through the astonishing victory of Christ's rising
again, clearly wholly transformed their everyday living;
for here was power. Power in no worldly kind, but in the
most far-reaching way of all: power in confronting all the
threats and distresses of existence in 'a sure and certain

hope'. 'He that has the Son, has life', as the Gospel of John puts it. *Has* life; a present experience of rescue which will never be taken away. Christians do not simply believe in life after death, but have the foretaste of it (what is sometimes referred to as 'realised eschatology') here and now. And experiencing that certainty carries with it a way of living. As Bishop Peter Selby has put it:

> The promise of universal rescue was the day-to-day experience of the earliest believers. . . . That experience was to be not something they had planned and executed for themselves, but the gift of the future which had been promised, and which Jesus had bestowed by his life and his death. For that day-to-day experience only one explanation could do justice, namely that the Jesus who had been dead was in truth alive, his appearance to those who had seen him now confirmed and given meaning by the reality of promise fulfilled. . . . Faith in Jesus, therefore, [inspired and] required the continual practice of the life of promise. . . . And the practice of the promise of rescue is what is asked for from the Christian community [today]; it includes the experience of what is to come, and a continued, active, waiting for it.

Eternal life, that mystery and promise of the future beyond that primary Last Thing, death, is something we are given a taste of (which is literally what the Biblical term 'foretaste' means) here and now, through the presence and power of Christ in our daily living, and through the many, many ways in which we experience the grace of God in signs of love. Our hope, that is, is rooted in the very nature of God himself, in the fact of the Resurrection, in what we know he has done in Christ in dealing with the sin that destroys us, and in our experience of that power of saving love in our lives, confirming to our hearts that we are children of God, and so 'heirs – heirs of God and co-heirs with Christ' (Romans 8:17).

And after death, the judgement

But, we ask fearfully, who decides whether my longing to
be with Christ for ever will be rewarded? I may respond
to God's offer, through Christ, to make me holy – for that
is the only holiness I can achieve – but who decides, and
how, what my future is on the other side of death? And so
we come to that Last Thing, the judgement. And our
minds and imaginations are full of the apocalyptic pictures in Scripture and in medieval art of what or how that
judgement may be. For, if the hope of the righteous (the
people of God) is resurrection, Scripture powerfully
affirms that the wicked are also raised, and that together
all experience judgement. Indeed, Jesus' own parables
clearly suggest a final discerning, a stripping away of
false self-perceptions, as an essential part of God's dealings with us as his glorious kingdom, of truth and justice
and mercy and compassion and light and joy, comes to
fruition. Clearly there can be no place in such a kingdom
for self-delusion, bolstered as it so often is by the projection onto others of the violence, destructiveness and
untruth we cannot face within ourselves. What then is our
hope, under what Iris Murdoch once called the 'just and
loving gaze' of such Truth?

Our hope begins with the love of God. He 'does not
delight in the death of sinners', but in their rescue into an
eternity of joyful relationship with him. The God who
sent his only Son into the world for us all is not the kind
of deity who of his own desire and for his own gratifica-
tion sentences them to outer darkness for ever. And so the
first thing we must remind ourselves of, to get the whole
thing in clear perspective, is that judgement is as indis-
solubly linked with hope of heaven, as with fear of hell.
We have seriously diminished the wonder of the justice of

God by thinking of Judgement Day almost exclusively in terms of wrath, in terms of punishment and condemnation. For the wonder of the justice of God is that in it the maintaining of the right is exactly balanced with the exercise of mercy: in it 'mercy and truth are met together, righteousness and peace have kissed each other' (Psalm 85:10, AV). That is where it is so very different from human justice, which usually errs on the one side or the other, the punitive or the indulgent. Therefore, God's court of judgement is indeed a place of holy awe; but that awe is not least because in it we shall see put right all that has been wrong. There will be a 'setting right' such that we shall at one and the same time have a profound experience of justice having been done and yet mercy flowing. Our guarantee of that is that we do not present ourselves naked (that is where the medieval pictures got it so wrong). Rather we appear in that court clothed in the grace of the Lord Jesus Christ, under whose name we stand; and 'spoken for' by him, whose credentials cover our own lack.

Scripture assures us of this. But we can go further. For Jesus made it very clear that in a real sense his presence on earth was both ushering in – 'beginning', so to speak – the kingdom, and therefore ushering in also the judgement. God's court of justice, in one sense, began its sitting with Jesus' presence among us. 'Now is the time for judgment on this world; now the prince of this world will be driven out,' he is recorded as saying (John 12:31). When he was on trial before Pilate, the political and judiciary orders of humanity were under judgement. When he was on trial before the Sanhedrin, the religious institutions of humanity were under judgement. For in his presence – whoever and whatever we are – we are judged. We are judged by the grace of his words, we are judged by the power of his healing acts, we are judged by the obedience of his life, we are judged above all by the wonder of his self-sacrifice in death.

What then of the belief we affirm in our Creeds: 'We believe that he will come again to judge the living and the dead'? Does not this bring together our experience of being judged by his presence among us here, in the local particularity of our day and time, with the vastness of that final ordering which we have glimpsed is our future and that of the cosmos? All human destiny, all Creation's destiny, is centred on Christ himself. Therefore, 'When God re-makes the world as he has promised, Christ will be personally present as the living heart and focus of all.' 'Look,' says Scripture, 'he is coming with the clouds, and every eye will see him' (Revelation 1:7).

But what we need to grasp is that all the pictures we are given of the Second Coming and the judgement which follows are attempts to express the truth that the glory of that coming will be a manifestation, a demonstrating to us, a showing, a presenting, in this world, of what is already true in heaven. (By 'heaven' is meant here the dimensions of reality immediate to God. I'll have more to say on that later.) For among 'angels and archangels and all the company of heaven' evil is already judged and banished, defeated, quenched; the reign of justice is already established, love is already unchallenged as the mode of being, fear and sorrow and crying are already no more, and all that would threaten and destroy is gone. Such a future is ours, and it is the Last Judgement which will usher it in.

... And hell

But, of course, what I have just described involves the exclusion of certain modes of being. That this is a spiritual reality, we have all experienced to some degree, however small. Saying 'yes' to God means saying 'no' to something else; it means excluding from my way of life habits of being and attitudes of heart which do not accord with 'love, joy, peace' – the signs on earth of the culture of heaven. And this helps us to begin to understand this next Biblical sign of 'the End', hell.

How may we think of hell? What do we believe about it? Scripture is very clear about its reality. It must not be understated, trivialised or ignored. But when we are considering the Biblical accounts of hell, it is important not to confuse the vivid descriptions that the ideas come dressed in, with the realities they express. The Bible often employs picture language or temporal imagery in its teaching, and it is a mistake to confuse the husk with the kernel. Keeping this in mind, then, what pictures does Scripture use to convey to us the reality of that which we call hell?

One vivid picture is of the rubbish heap of Jerusalem, *Gehinnom*, where the purifying flames were maintained day and night. Its derivative name, 'Gehenna', thus became powerfully symbolic through two millennia of Christian culture of eternal damnation and everlasting agony. To choose hell, therefore, is to choose the rubbish heap, the place of thrown-away things, with all the pain associated with waste. Dante's *Inferno*, Elgar's *Dream of Gerontius*, and William Golding's *Darkness Visible* all draw on this image, as do countless medieval and Renaissance paintings.

A second picture is of eternal separation from God our Father, chained down in separateness so that there is no release from it. (So in Jesus' parable of Dives and Lazarus.) The image is terrible in its desolation of loneliness and finality. The theme is expressed with sad beauty and poignancy in Michelangelo's *Last Judgement*, on the ceiling of the Sistine Chapel in Rome.

A third image is of the end of the battle between good and evil, between God and the epitome of the powers of evil, named in Scripture as 'Satan' or the Devil. Pictures of this can be seen in many early Christian frescoes, from the third century onwards. This particular representation resonates with many thinkers (even agnostic ones) because of its marked emphasis on our world as answering to moral laws, where good and evil, right and wrong, endure as absolute truths which affect human destiny. In that sense the world is a battleground between two forces, in an unrelenting fight which will only end when Christ returns in glory, and the promise of his kingdom of justice and love is fulfilled. Then, in this Scripture image, will come the Judgement, when Satan and all the forces of evil will be judged and sentenced, and banished to hell.

For some, such a picture is invalid because of its personalising of evil in the figure of Satan; it seems a crude, mythological concept with no right place in modern thought. Such debate can distract us from the essence of the image, which is that every Christian, and the Church as a whole, is in battle against the power of evil. Military theorists are aware that when it comes to battle you need to listen to your front-line troops because they are actually engaged with the enemy. So, with respect to the Church, we need to listen carefully not only to our philosophers and theologians in their exploration of modes of thought, but to the testimony of those who live on the frontiers of the world, in direct engagement. Such testimony tells of a universal encounter with evil which echoes the teaching of Scripture. So, even allowing for the fact that our world-view is necessarily different from that of the New

Testament, we should not lightly devalue the Bible's pictures of the realities after which we are grasping. As C. S. Lewis once said, 'I have always gone as close to dualism as the New Testament allows, and, believe me, it allows us to get very close.'

What is common to the three descriptions of hell I have mentioned is the note of separation, of grieving, of anguished regret. Of the mysteries of God's ultimate judging of others none of us is finally qualified to speak. What Scripture very clearly teaches, and our personal experience of the life of faith and obedience confirms, is that we each have the capacity to sentence ourselves to separation, even eternal separation, from the One who loves us eternally. For heaven requires consent: no one can be compulsorily installed there. As Helen Oppenheimer points out, God is not like 'a mythical mother at the sea-side: "I brought you here to enjoy yourselves, and enjoy yourselves you shall!"' For heaven is about being in love in a way analogous with the phrase as we currently use it. That is, wanting to be with the one loved, wholly absorbed in thought and imagination with delight that the loved one exists and exists in special, unique relationship to me. So it is between us and God, in the mode of being which will be heaven. And such love can, of course, never be forced. Just as between human beings, so between God and each of us, we choose to respond to the experience of love he offers. Freedom is a condition of true love – even in our limited human way of offering and receiving it. How much more then is this true of the love relationship with God? Just so, we can choose (and most of us have done so at some moment in our lives) to exclude ourselves from the heaven of his reciprocated love and place ourselves in the hell of separation from him. Even brief experiences of that, before we 'come to ourselves' (see Luke 15:17) and rush back to our Lord, give us a terrifying glimpse of what the hell of eternal separation from God might be.

And yet even here there is the mystery of the infinite love of God. For how can we begin to sound the depths of what it means – what profound consequences it has for our ultimate happiness – that God's love has literally gone to hell and back for us? Though it is absolutely true, as some have put it, that 'dogmatic universalism contradicts the very nature of love', and love 'will not, because it cannot, compel the surrender of a single heart that holds out against it', yet the mysterious reality is that hell itself, that mode of being which is lost in utter separateness, has known the blessing and power of the presence of the Lord Jesus. He freely chose, out of love, to search even the darkness of that way of being. 'He descended into hell': that place of utter estrangement from his Father God, and ours. 'For the sake of the love which was his nature, God in Jesus chose to know the darkness of the utter absence of love.' No wonder the heavens shook and the Earth erupted and it was dark! The silence of Holy Saturday addresses our terror at the thought of hell and says, 'If I descend into the depths, Thou art there also. . . .'

And so, before I leave this and turn to the wonders of God's proposed destiny for us, there are just three further notes I want to sound. First – as will be clear from all I have said above – *we need not, indeed must not, live with fear.* I remember how as a young curate I was called upon to help a man who lived with a daily terror of hell. When he was a child, his parents had night after night warned him over-vividly of the consequences of sin; and so, though he knew of the mercies of God, they were not equally present to his imagination, and he could not turn his back on the horrors of hell. Yet 'perfect love casts out fear', and the

keynote of our approach to the mystery of this particular
Last Thing must be the taking hold in confidence of the
truth that God forgives – has forgiven already – those who
come to him.

My second 'footnote' grows out of that. *The Church
must not terrify people into heaven.* It is 'the love of Christ
[which] constrains us', and that, not terror, is what we
offer to those with whom we speak of Jesus. Of course we
cannot and must not fail to speak truly of what separateness from God means; but this is so that people grasp the
reality of choice within which we live. A choice between
the fullness of delight in living with God, loved and
loving; or in rejecting all that that means. Faithful witness
focuses on the love of God which is the inspiration for following and obedience – not the terrors of eternal separation from God.

And finally, all that I have said above leads me to
emphasise again that *the gospel teaches hope, not despair.* A
hope grounded not in ourselves and our own frail
natures, but in all that we have learned and seen of the
nature of our God and his work for us through his Son,
our Lord Jesus Christ. As the hymn puts it:

> There's a wideness in God's mercy
> like the wideness of the sea;
> there's a kindness in his justice
> which is more than liberty.

And verse 3 continues:

> For the love of God is broader
> than the measures of man's mind;
> and the heart of the Eternal
> is most wonderfully kind.
>
> F. W. Faber

The Communion of Saints

Before we look, finally, at the last of the Last Things, heaven itself, I want to explore a little with you of what we understand as Christians by 'the Communion of Saints', for this is where the life of eternity and our present life in the world explicitly meet.

For in our worship together as Church we regularly express our strong sense that the worship we offer is set within the worship offered by fellow believers on the other side of death; offering our Holy Communion 'with angels and archangels and all the company of heaven'. In our Creeds we affirm our belief in 'the Communion of Saints'. *What* do we believe?

We believe, as the Bible affirms, that God 'is not the God of the dead, but of the living' (Luke 20:38); so that, as Jesus said, Abraham and Isaac and Jacob were presently alive even as Moses faced the burning bush and called upon *their* God; so that, as Peter, John and James saw, Moses and Elijah were presently alive as they appeared on the mountain of the Transfiguration in converse with Jesus. That is, though there is some final consummation and transformation to which pictures of the Last Day look forward, yet that foretaste of which I have spoken, of eternal life which is already ours, is a sharing in the present resurrection life of those who have gone before us. We may be sure of this because when Christians die, they die 'in Christ'; that is, they die sharing in the common life of the body of Christ which is the company of believers. Since death is defeated they are thus 'brought home to the Father and to that eternal life which is Christ's gift and promise'. They remain 'in Christ', just as we their successors are 'in Christ': our fellowship reaches across the divide of the grave by virtue of the shared quality of eternal life we have in him.

So we are, Paul reminds us, surrounded by a 'great cloud of witnesses' (Hebrews 12:1) who encourage us on our journey. I have found it a great encouragement to know I am united in Christ with other Archbishops of Canterbury who sought to serve Christ as whole-heartedly as I am attempting to do. And for you, my dear friends of the future, there will be another Archbishop of Canterbury with whom, in both this world and that to come, I in my turn shall be united in Christ. As the one Church of Jesus spans time and eternity, so those who have passed through the grave before us are in the Communion of Saints still part of the mission of Christ, and aid us by their love and our common allegiance to our Lord.

And an essential part of this mission is prayer. With the Communion of Saints we are united in a common praise and intercession; and even to those for whom prayers for the dead are unacceptable, this sense of unitedness in praise must surely be of importance – indeed our liturgies declare it.

Here I have to confess that in my early days I myself could not accept prayers or intercession for the dead as a valid activity, since they might seem to undercut the effi-cacy of Christ's death. (If in the life to come I am in the immediate presence of Christ, surely there seems no need for others to pray for me!) But over the years, as I began to think more deeply about what we mean by 'the Communion of Saints', I have begun to see that my fears were groundless. If I treasure and depend upon the prayer of my fellow Christians with me in this life, then how much richer this is when I understand it as part of a vast and unceasing movement of prayer which crosses the thin dividing waters of death. For as we remember our forerunners in thankfulness, and share with them in praise to God and intercession for the world, so our prayers for them twine with theirs for us, all of them contained within the prayer of praise to God which is Christ's alone. In Christ – and only in Christ – I can call upon the strengthening of the Holy Spirit as seen in the faithfulness of St Augustine, first Archbishop of Canterbury; the spirituality of St Anselm; the courage of Thomas Cranmer; the social commitment of William Temple; and beyond these the gentle obedience of the Virgin Mary, and the fire and boldness of all the saints of the Church. All these share our life and offering of prayer, and are thus, as in this life we are to each other, a spiritual resource and succour to the Church Militant.

Such mutuality of prayer affirms our certainty that those who have died are in the hands of God, and their destiny is shaped by his good purposes. For the same reason, our litany includes prayers for 'those whose faith is known to God alone'. For Scripture says clearly that God created, loves and sustains the whole of humanity; and that Christ died for the 'sins of the whole world'. Since our prayers, across the divide of death, are joined together through being in Christ, to intercede for all is clearly within the will and according to the purpose of the Father God.

I ought here to add very briefly the rider that it is prayer *with* the saints of which I speak, not prayer to them. (Although I must affirm that many Catholic friends who pray *to* the Virgin Mary and to the saints of the Church are not ignoring Christ as the only way to the Father. Rather, they see such prayers as a continuum that runs from the Cross.) Nevertheless, only when we remember that it is *God* to whom we are turning in our prayers, whatever the route we use, will those prayers be properly directed. For only in Christ can the mystery of prayerful relations between the living and the departed find full and right expression. And so it is in Christ that the communion of loving fellowship we know together in this life as fellow believers is extended into a loving fellowship which includes the whole Communion of Saints.

The surprises of heaven

I've said that our belief in our future destiny is one of hope, with the securest possible grounds for it; and I do most strongly, my dear friends of the future, urge the truth of this upon you, whatever the pressures on your faith and the cataclysms you may in your generation be facing. For what is the destiny for which this whole story of Christian belief I have shared with you, the belief which binds together your generation with mine, and with those before me and with those coming after you – what is the *point*, the purpose, of this story of the 'things we have most surely believed'? This story, 'anchored in the Bible, taught by the Church, related to our culture, and relevant for life'? Is it not that God has created us with a purpose, that we should live with him and enjoy him for ever? And this is no picture of static perfection, but of the delighted exploration in love for ever of the inexhaustible riches of his nature.

But what do we believe this means? How may the troubled heart of contemporary unbelief contemplate 'a new heaven and a new earth'? What are we to understand by it? Helen Oppenheimer, in her glorious chapter on 'Glibness, Gloom and Glory', helps us in the face of such questions:

If Christianity is the truth, one would expect there to be a kind of felicity which has a characteristic that is hard to pin down and easy to caricature, which might be called 'beyond-ness'. If this is just 'pie in the sky' after all, it will be no more than an unworthy projection of earthly satisfactions. Rather, it needs to be a happiness dependent on death and resurrec-tion. To die is to surrender oneself . . . What is promised is that on the other side of such surrender, not instead of it, there is to be a rising again. Christians can expect to find blessing, satisfaction, fulfilment on the other side of whatever there may be to face and undergo, including death itself.

So we have to approach these mysteries with the agnosti-cism of true reverence: we simply cannot envisage what these marvellous new realities will be. What we do have, as with the other Last Things, is a series of pictures, images, descriptions in Scripture which are attempts to show inspired glimpses people have had of what heaven will be like. It will, for instance, be like a city, but a city of the most unimaginably beautiful kind, inhabited in joy and harmony by a community bound together in delight and joy in their Lord. A community. For the judgement, the Bible insists, is about nations as well as individuals; about what a people might become when the earthly experience of being a 'covenanted people' is transmuted into the ultimacy of the coming together from every nation and people of the one gathered community of heaven. As nations we are judged by that future, but as nations we are also redeemed into it.

Or, there is the picture of heaven as a wedding feast with – oh, wonder – ourselves sharing the very centre of the joy, as a bride does with the groom. And in this picture the groom is Christ, and – in the language of wedding imagery – we are to be united with him for ever in an eter-nity of unspoiled delight. For 'we shall be made like him' – fitted at last to share fully his life. And so the ultimate point of this story is unfolded before us: we shall, in our earthly life through the Spirit and in the life to come by union with our Lord, grow into his likeness so that we shall participate in the life of God himself – what the theologians call *theosis*. Sharing in the divine nature, we shall be 'transformed into his likeness with ever-increasing glory' (2 Corinthians 3:18).

These are concepts almost beyond the reach of our fingertips, pictures which are like a kaleidoscope, changing and shifting because beyond our focus. Yet each generation has found ways of retelling this bit of the story. I hope, for instance, that John Bunyan's *The Pilgrim's Progress* is still available to you (electronically or even on good old-fashioned paper) so that you, like us, can revel in his seventeenth-century version of the wonders of heaven, rooted in the Bible's pictures as it is. But here is an account in my own day, from Golding's novel about a man, a novelist, who has been in a flight of penitence and shame from the 'great Recorder' who will show him in judgement the Book of his life. He has finally taken refuge in a hotel in Rome, where one hot afternoon he has a vision. He thinks he sees God standing on the top of the church opposite his balcony window, where 'he could simply step across the roof and collect me'. And then suddenly he seems to be standing on the roof with God, looking down at the steps below . . .

There was sunlight everywhere, not the heavy light of Rome, but a kind of radiance as if the sun were everywhere. . . . I saw that the steps had the symmetrical curve of a musical instrument, guitar, cello, violin. But this harmonious shape was now embellished and interrupted everywhere by the people and the flowers and the glitter of jewels strewn among them on the steps. All the people were young and like flowers. I found that God was standing by me on the roof of his house, and we went down together and stood among the people with the pattern of jewels and the heaps of flowers all blazing inside and out with the radiance. Then they made music of the steps. They held hands and moved and the movement was music. I saw they were neither male nor female or perhaps they were both and it was of no importance. What mattered was the music they made. . . .

There were steps going down, narrow steps to a door with a drumhead. We went through. I think that there was a dark calm sea beyond it, since I have nothing to speak with but metaphor. Also there were creatures in the sea that sang. For the singing and the song I have no words at all.

One man's pictures, from my own century, of the inexpressible, of the 'new heaven and the new earth' that is promised, and of our life together with God in that new creation. Because that heaven in one sense already exists, in the purpose and will of God, the nature of final events may well be the fusion of this life with the life of God as the temporal is embraced with the eternal and the natural transformed by the spiritual. Whatever the future holds, of this we can be quite sure: God's Creation is set not for dissolution but for transmutation in glory. 'The creation itself will be set free from its bondage to decay and will obtain the freedom of the glory of the children of God' (Romans 8:21, NRSV). Then, in the majesty and wonder of Christ's personal return to us, and the marvels that follow, we shall find ourselves experiencing something like that which C. S. Lewis described in the final paragraph of his prophetic children's book, *The Last Battle*:

The things that began to happen after that were so great and beautiful that I cannot write them. And for us this is the end of all stories, and we can most truly say that they all lived happily ever after. But for them it was only the beginning of the real story. All their life in this world . . . had only been the cover and the title page: now at last they were beginning

Chapter One of the Great Story which no-one on earth has read: which goes on for ever: in which every chapter is better than the one before.

'In which every chapter is better than the one before' . . . And so it must be. For we have reached the moment beyond which we cannot go and I can say no more because this, truly, is about the future. But as I finish this final Letter from the See of Canterbury, I know that when you and I, dear friends of the future, have entered into the full wonder of those things I have described in it, we shall have 'merrily met in heaven'; and for you, as for me, God will – at last – be all in all.

Yours in the wonder and certainty of that hope,

Bibliography

Books referred to include the following:

INTRODUCTION

H. D. Carberry, 'Epitaph', *This Day and Age*, ed. Hewett, Edward Arnold, 1960

LETTER 1

Dr Richard McBrien, *Essays in Theology*, published 26th January 1996, USA

Doctrine Commission of the Church of England, *Christian Believing*, Church House Publishing, 1976

LETTER 2

Sir Arthur Wolfendale, 'The Evolution of the Universe

and the Evolution of Belief', *My Journey, Your Journey*, ed. Pearson, Lion, 1996

Samuel Beckett, *Waiting for Godot*, Faber and Faber, 1956

LETTER 3

Paul Davies/John Gribbin, *The Matter Myth: Towards 21st Century Science*, Viking, 1991

Arthur Jones, 'Whose side is Science on?' *Third Way*, April 1996

Saul Bellow, *Mr Sammler's Planet*, Weidenfeld and Nicolson, 1970

LETTER 4

C. S. Lewis, Sonnet, 'He whom I bow to only knows to whom I bow', in *The Pilgrim's Regress*, 1st edition 1933; quoted from Eerdman's Pocket Version, 1977

Robert Herrick, 'To Keep a True Lent', in *The Faber Book of Religious Verse*, ed. Helen Gardner, Faber, 1972

Dag Hammerskjöld, *Markings*, trans. Leif Sjoborg and W. H. Auden, Faber and Faber, 1964

LETTER 5

Eric Mascall, *Jesus: Who He Is and How We Know Him*, Darton, Longman and Todd, 1985

Albert Schweitzer, *The Quest for the Historical Jesus*

N. T. Wright, *Who Was Jesus?*, SPCK, 1994

LETTER 6

Michael Ramsey, *The Glory of God and the Transfiguration of Christ*, Longman Green, 1949

LETTER 7

Austin Farrer, in *Kerygma and Myth*, Vol. I, ed. H. W. Bartoch, SPCK, 1953

Geza Vermes, *Jesus the Jew*, Collins, 1973

Doctrine Commission, *The Mystery of Salvation*, Church House Publishing, 1995

Helen Oppenheimer, *The Hope of Happiness*, SCM, 1983

LETTER 8

Doctrine Commission, *The Mystery of Salvation*, as above

William Golding, *Darkness Visible*, Faber, 1979

Albert Camus, *The Plague*, trans. Stewart Gilbert, Penguin, 1948

Anon, 'The Dream of the Rood', in *The Anglo-Saxon World*, ed. and transl. by Kevin Crossley-Holland, OUP, 1984

W. H. Vanstone, in *Love's Endeavour, Love's Expense*, Darton, Longman and Todd, 1977

LETTER 9

Edmund Hill, *The Mystery of the Trinity*, Geoffrey Chapman, 1985

Doctrine Commission, *We Believe in the Holy Spirit*, Church House Publishing, 1991

LETTER 10

John Polkinghorne, *Serious Talk*, SCM, 1995

Peter Selby, *Rescue*, SPCK, 1995

Helen Oppenheimer, as above

William Golding, *The Paper Men*, Faber, 1984